Lecture Notes in Computer Science 3811

Commenced Publication in 1973
Founding and Former Series Editors:
Gerhard Goos, Juris Hartmanis, and Jan van Leeuwen

T0232832

Christoph Bussler   Ming-Chien Shan (Eds.)

Technologies
for E-Services

6th International Workshop, TES 2005
Trondheim, Norway, September 2-3, 2005
Revised Selected Papers

 Springer

Volume Editors

Christoph Bussler
Cisco Systems, Inc.
3600 Cisco Way, MS SJC18/2/4, San Jose, CA 95134, USA
E-mail: chbussler@aol.com

Ming-Chien Shan
HP Labs
13264 Glasgow Court, Saratoga, CA 95070, USA
E-mail: MingChien.Shan@mail.com

Library of Congress Control Number: 2006920029

CR Subject Classification (1998): H.2, H.4, C.2, H.3, J.1, K.4.4, I.2.11

LNCS Sublibrary: SL 3 – Information Systems and Application, incl. Internet/Web
and HCI

ISSN   0302-9743
ISBN-10   3-540-31067-3 Springer Berlin Heidelberg New York
ISBN-13   978-3-540-31067-9 Springer Berlin Heidelberg New York

Springer is a part of Springer Science+Business Media

springer.com

© Springer-Verlag Berlin Heidelberg 2006
Printed in Germany

Typesetting: Camera-ready by author, data conversion by Scientific Publishing Services, Chennai, India
Printed on acid-free paper   SPIN: 11607380   06/3142   5 4 3 2 1 0

Preface

The 6th Workshop on Technologies for E-Services (TES-05) was held September 2-3, 2005, in conjunction with the 31st International Conference on Very Large Data Bases (VLDB 2005) in Trondheim, Norway.

The next generation of applications will be developed in the form of services that are offered over a network, either a company's intranet or the Internet. Service-based architectures depend on an infrastructure that allows service providers to describe and advertise their services and service consumers to discover and select the services that best fulfill their requirements. Frameworks and messaging protocols for e-services in stationary and mobile environments are being developed and standardized, metadata and ontologies are being defined, and mechanisms are under development for service composition, delivery, monitoring, and payment. End-to-end security and quality of service guarantees will be essential for the acceptance of e-services. As e-services become pervasive, e-service management will play a central role.

The workshop's objective is to provide a forum for researchers and practitioners to present new developments and experience reports. The goal of the TES workshop is to identify the technical issues, models, and infrastructures that enable enterprises to provide e-services to other businesses and individual customers.

In response to the call for submissions, 40 papers were submitted, out of which the Program Committee selected 10 high-quality submissions for presentation at the workshop. Unfortunately, one author had to withdraw, and the remaining nine papers that were presented are included in these proceedings.

The workshop itself started with a keynote given by Umeshwar Dayal on "Optimization of Business Processes (& Composite E-Services)." He gave interesting insights into past, current, and future developments in the area of business process management and the application of these results to composite e-services. Afterwards the three technical sessions "Design," "Technology," and "Composite Web Services" took place and very interesting and stimulating research paper presentations were delivered, resulting in many questions and discussions.

We would like to thank the authors for their submissions to the workshop, the Program Committee for their hard work during a very brief reviewing period, the keynote speaker and presenters for their very interesting presentations, and the audience for their interest, questions, and discussions.

September 2004

Christoph Bussler
Ming-Chien Shan

Workshop Organization Committee

Christoph Bussler
Digital Enterprise Research Institute (DERI), Ireland

Ming-Chien Shan
Hewlett-Packard Laboratories, CA, USA

Program Committee

Boualem Benatallah
Fabio Casati
Emilia Cimpian
Jen-Yao Chung
Francisco Curbera
Marlon Dumas
Schahram Dustdar
Timothy Finin
Dimitrios Georgakopoulos
Paul Grefen
Juan Gomez
Armin Haller
Manfred Hauswirth
Kashif Iqbal
Mick Kerrigan
Jacek Kopecky
Frank Leymann
Adrian Mocan
Heiko Ludwig

Eyal Oren
Cesare Pautasso
Mike Papazoglou
Barbara Pernici
Krithi Ramamritham
Manfred Reichert
Dumitru Roman
Brahmananda Sapkota
Karsten Schulz
Amit Sheth
Thomas Strang
Katia Sycara
Farouk Toumani
Kunal Verma
Michal Zaremba
Liang-Jie Zhang
Michal Zaremba
Lizhu Zhou

Table of Contents

Table of Contents

Challenges in Business Process Analysis
and Optimization

Malu Castellanos, Fabio Casati, Mehmet Sayal, and Umeshwar Dayal

Hewlett-Packard Laboratories, Palo Alto, CA
firstname.lastname@hp.com

Abstract. As organizations become more and more process-centered and as
the extended enterprise becomes more of a reality, there is an increasing need
to move towards the intelligent enterprise characterized by its agility for provisioning resources and services and the adaptation and optimization of its
business processes. Many are the challenges that need to be faced to equip the
extended enterprise with intelligence, in particular with business process
intelligence. In this paper we present an overview of some challenges, opportunities and directions for analysis and optimization of business processes
towards the intelligent enterprise.

1 Business Process Intelligence

Over the years the concept of *enterprise* has evolved dramatically as its functionalities
and boundaries have extended in response to business and technological changes. The
traditional monolithic enterprise was characterized by all of its operations being performed in-house, and as a consequence, the key challenges addressed by the enterprise
in the 1980's were functional automation and enterprise integration. Competitive pres-
sures in the 1990's and early 2000's have compelled enterprises to outsource many of
their non-core operations such as financial processing or even manufacturing. Advances
in network technology, information exchange standards and middleware have made it
possible to reach beyond the boundaries of the traditional enterprise to integrate trading
partners, suppliers, and service providers giving rise to the *extended* enterprise. B2B
frameworks and protocols (such as Oasis/ebXML and RosettaNet) have emerged for
partner integration and the management of collaborative business processes across the
extended enterprise. The high complexity of the extended enterprise has made it crucial
to devise ways of operating and managing its components and interactions in an automatic, efficient and flexible way. In particular, integration of information and process
flows, agile provisioning of resources and services, monitoring, analysis, adaptation and
optimization of business processes are characteristic of a new concept of enterprise, the
intelligent enterprise.

There are many challenges to make the enterprise transformation a reality. Architecture and infrastructure for its ecosystem; modeling of collaborative, inter-organizational
business processes that span the partners in the extended enterprise; description, composition, publishing, registration and discovery of business service providers; rapid and
dynamic connection and disconnection of partners; security and trust; and negotiation to

C. Bussler and M.-C. Shan (Eds.): TES 2005, LNCS 3811, pp. 1–10, 2006.
© Springer-Verlag Berlin Heidelberg 2006

name a few. In this paper, we focus on aspects related to the management and optimization of business processes in the intelligent enterprise.

Our key thesis in this paper is that an (extended) enterprise is an entity that delivers services to customers, and it is the business processes underlying such services which drive the enterprise (Figure 1). Traditional business process management supports the definition, execution and monitoring of business processes, defines and controls the sequence, timing and other dependencies among tasks, enforces business rules and policies, assigns resources (humans, data, applications, web services) to individual tasks, monitors and tracks all aspects of the process execution. Inter-enterprise business process management extends the above functionalities to the extended enterprise as a result of the marriage between process management and web services technologies. In the intelligent enterprise business process management is equipped with functionalities that facilitate the optimization of the quality (in terms of metrics meaningful to the enterprise –internal quality-, or to the customers –external quality-) of intra- and inter-enterprise business processes. This is known as *Business Process Intelligence*.

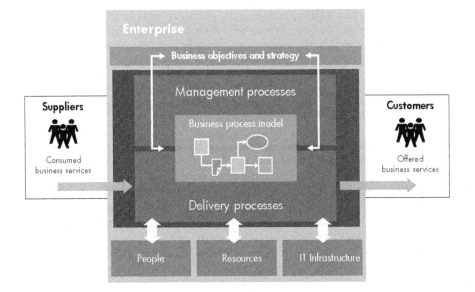

Fig. 1. Business processes drive the Enterprise

In business process intelligence, quality metrics can be computed from process execution data logged in various forms (workflow engine logs, web service execution logs, application logs, event logs, etc). For example, the performance metric of an order process could be derived from the start and end times of execution of orders processed during a given period of time. By warehousing [Bonifati01] the execution data and the metrics the business process can be monitored, analyzed and optimized with different kinds of techniques relying on data mining, statistics, simulation, and optimization, among others [Castellanos05C]. The purpose of this paper is to discuss opportunities for analysis and optimization of business processes along with some directions and challenges. In particular, we discuss six challenging areas: process validation, resource allocation, service selection, work queue management, time-based correlation, and prediction and proactive optimization.

2 Process Validation

Business processes underlying enterprise business operations often start with a model (composed by individual tasks along with their order and dependencies) that is mapped to the IT infrastructure to be implemented accordingly. Unfortunately, it is often the case that the initial alignment of the process model and its implementation doesn't last too long, sooner or later the implementation starts to deviate from the model in response to changes in the infrastructure or in the business objectives of the enterprise. New steps and even paths can be added to handle new situations and exceptions, conditions in the decisions may be modified to adapt to new requirements for following one path or another, steps could be merged in response to some changes in the organization, and so on. At some point nobody knows what is the 'real' process and what deviations have taken place. Moreover, the deviations can occur only for some process executions without anybody knowing in which cases or contexts this occurs.

The misalignment between the real process and its original model needs to be resolved in a number of situations. To optimize a process or simply improve its operation, it is necessary to have a clear picture of the model as it is executed in practice. When the process has been subject to changes over time, it is even more important to analyze how such changes or deviations are affecting its performance and what are the opportunities to improve it. In addition, new legislations such as Sarbanes-Oxley, require to document processes and add controls where appropriate. For this, it is necessary to find the deviations that have happened and obtain a process model that corresponds to the reality. Monitoring is yet another activity that requires checking the consistency between the analyst's high level view and the actual process. Finally, by identifying process model deviations it is possible to perform sensitivity analysis to analyze alternatives to such deviations.

Triggered by situations like the aforementioned, research has started in this direction under the name of process validation, process alignment, delta analysis and conformance testing. It basically consists of assessing whether a process model actually corresponds to what is executed by a company's IT infrastructure and in identifying the deviations if that is not the case. This is related to the area of process discovery which elicits the process model from the logged execution data when such a model does not exist. In contrast, in process validation the model already exists and it is the deviations from it what is of interest. In both cases it is the event, transaction or audit log what is mined to discover how the process is being conducted in reality. This kind of log typically records events that correspond to the start and completion of activities in the IT infrastructure. In addition, the log entry provides information about the task identifier and about the process execution identifier in the context of which the task is being performed. As an example, an entry in the log could say that an 'inventory check' step started at 3.30pm and completed at 4.15 pm, and that it has been executed in the context of order processing #539 (where 'order processing' is the process type whose model we want to verify, while #539 identifies a specific execution - also called case or instance - of the process). Different products like WFMS,

ERPs, transaction monitor systems like HP OVTA, HP BPI, to name a few, provide this kind of log.

A few techniques have been proposed to validate processes and most of them consist of applying process discovery to learn the 'real' model [Aalst03] and then compare it with the original one to identify deviations and measure the degree of (mis)alignment [Rozinat05]. The challenge remains in developing alternative techniques that do not require discovering the real model so that the cost of verification is lower while at the same time gaining more efficiency. Furthermore, to make things more versatile and automatic, research needs to be done for techniques that could keep track of deviations from a process model as they occur, associate them to their context, and suggest changes to the model as more evidence of these deviations is collected.

3 Resource Allocation

A business process is formally defined as a sequence of tasks which are carried out by resources. The resources that are in charge of executing the individual process tasks can be humans, software applications, or web services. The allocation of resources to tasks can be done in either static or dynamic manner. Static resource allocation means that a pre-defined set of assignments between resources and tasks is applied and stays fixed for all instances (executions) of the business process. A dynamic allocation allows the process designers to define resource pools, which contain resources that are capable of carrying out a particular task or a set of tasks, and the actual assignment is done during the execution of each individual process instance. The concept of *Virtual Resources* is generally used for defining such resource pools.

The allocation of resources to tasks can significantly affect the performance and outcome of the business processes, which in turn affects the quality of services and products of an enterprise. It is possible to allocate one or more resources from a virtual resource pool to a particular task. Identification of bottlenecks in a business process and proper allocation of resources to critical tasks can help a business meet the deadlines and Service Level Agreement (SLA) terms while delivering services and products at a desired quality.

Business process simulation tools are used for analyzing the behavior of resources and their affect on the overall performance and outcome of processes. Businesses often need to know what would be the effect on business goals (in terms of metrics) if certain process parameters would be set to different values. For example, it is important to know (or predict) the effect of assigning two resources to a particular task, instead of one. Sensitivity analysis (what-if analysis) allows users to analyze outcomes of various scenarios in which the effect of different parameter settings can be observed. It is important to know how much benefit such an additional resource allocation could bring. Possible parameters for simulation and sensitivity analysis could be resource pool sizes for individual tasks, inter-arrival rate of entities to be processed, resource behavior (response time to particular tasks), and cost of individual resources (per unit time or total). It is usually assumed that data needed for setting up simulation parameters is available from audit logs of Workflow Management Systems (WFMS). Most business process definitions in WFMS tools include explicit information about resource-task allocation. However, business processes are not always automated using

WFMS, and such allocation information is not usually available. Therefore, it is often necessary to extract resource allocation manually or automatically using various data analysis and mining techniques.

Businesses are interested not only in understanding the effect of changes in a process but also in determining the best possible allocation of resources in order to achieve certain performance and quality goals. Simulation leveraged with a search technique offers one solution [Castellanos05C]. Here, the objective could be to minimize the number of process instances that exceed a certain metric threshold or to maximize the overall value of a given metric. Other metrics that need to be kept within range would be the constraints and the maximum number of units in each resource pool would constitute the bounds of the search space. The challenge is how to take advantage of domain knowledge to quickly reduce the search space to minimize the number of resource allocation configurations that need to be simulated. Other techniques, such as mathematical programming, can be brought to bear on this problem.

It is also important to automatically identify the resources that perform poorly in certain contexts. Data mining, and in particular classification algorithms, can be used for this purpose [Casati04]. For example, a classification rule may indicate that involvement of a particular resource in task executions results in poor performance. Replacement of such a resource with another one from a resource pool may yield much better execution performance. Similarly, time-correlation detection [Sayal05] can tell us the time-dependent cause-effect relationships among any numeric variables (e.g., business metrics or operational data). As an example, a decrease in the performance of a particular resource may trigger the appearance of a bottleneck in a given critical step of a process after a certain time period. Automatic detection of such time-correlations can help business managers optimize resource allocation to proactively avoid such effects.

4 Service Selection

A related issue that can potentially affect the quality or performance of a business process is that of dynamic service selection, that is, of selecting at run-time the service that can best perform (implement) a certain step in the process. The lack of maturity and of standardization at the business level (that is, lack of standard business interfaces, protocols, and in general of high-level B2B standards) has made this problem to date irrelevant for the industry, where processes had to be implemented with a static binding to the services implementing the steps. However, lately we are witnessing an increased push not only to standardize low-level interaction protocols, but also protocols (and semantics) at the business level (e.g., what is the meaning of a *PurchaseOrder* document and how it should be exchanged among parties to arrive at a complete purchase transaction). This raises the possibility, and hence the opportunity, for dynamic service binding, at least between closed communities of trusted partners. Ideally, the goal is to select, at each step, the service that maximizes the probability of achieving certain quality of performance goals.

Many approaches to this problem exist, but they are mostly based on having providers define non-functional parameters that specify the cost, duration, and other *service quality metrics*. Then, for each step in the process execution, a choice is made about the provider to be used by matching desired and provided quality, or by computing some utility function over the service quality metrics, with the goal of achieving the best possible process execution "quality". This kind of approaches has several limitations. For example, it requires clients (the ones executing the process) to trust the accuracy of the metric values declared by the providers, it assumes the ability to identify the important service metrics that contribute to high process execution quality, it requires a standard way to model metrics so that customer and providers can understand each other, and it assumes that customers have a clear idea of how exactly process quality goals depend on (are a function of) the value of the providers' promised quality parameters. In general, these are not realistic assumptions. Hence, the challenge here is how to perform dynamic service selection without incurring in the limiting assumptions described above (which also require significant modeling efforts).

A possible solution consists in having customers define the quality goals of their business processes and then specify which past executions they consider to be of high quality. This can be done by either specifying a function over process execution data that labels process executions with quality measures (e.g., all invoice payment processes that completed before the payment due date are "good"), or by having customers explicitly label process executions, for example based on feedback collected online. Once the quality of past process executions are known or measurable, quality-labeled process execution data are mined to build a set of models that, at each stage during process execution and based on the specific characteristics of each process execution, identify the service provider that historically, in "analogous" situations, has contributed to high quality processes. This approach is feasible since it focuses on what users really care about, what is the overall quality of the process; it involves little modeling effort (defining process quality goals is the only effort needed by the customer); and it is not based on provider-defined non-functional parameters for each service, but rather based on facts, and can progressively adjust based on changing notions of process quality as well as on changing behavior of service providers. We refer the interested reader to [Casati04] for details.

5 Work Queue Management

Many business processes are characterized by manual steps, that is, steps executed by human users (called processors) rather than services. In some cases the step creates a work item which is assigned to a specific processor, while in others the item is placed in a shared work queue.

In both cases, processors have, at any given time, several work items on which they can work, often belonging to different process instances, and they typically have flexibility in selecting which one to process first. The problem here is how to find out which is the "optimal" order in which work items should be executed, where by optimal we mean the order that minimizes SLA violations, or the total penalties resulting from the SLA violations, or that optimize some user-defined performance function (that can for example take into account SLA violations, penalties, importance of the customers, etc..). Ideally, we are looking for techniques that prioritize the items in the work queues to optimize this user-defined function. For simplicity, we just assume that the goal is that of minimizing deadline expirations for the processes.

Leaving the decision of which work item to pick completely to the processor may lead to adverse consequences and to violations of SLAs. For example, the processors may start working on an item belonging to a process instance that is, performance-wise, on target, and neglect more urgent work.

Identifying such an optimal solution is however not trivial, and indeed simple approaches do not solve the problem. For example, simply selecting the "oldest" work item would be an incorrect approach, as SLA violations depend on the process duration not on the duration of each step. Even if the work item has been started long ago, we may be well in time to meet our deadlines. Selecting the work item corresponding to the instance closer to reaching its deadline also does not produce the desired result: if we are very close to the deadline already, we won't be able to finish in time anyway, and we may as well give higher priorities to work items of other process instances. In general, we have therefore to be aware of the expected durations of the forthcoming steps to assess what priority to give to a work item, and assess which priority order minimizes violations. Depending on the level of sophistication, we may use a simple average to derive the expected time, or we may use complex forecasting techniques that based on the characteristics of the specific process instance at hand, try to predict the duration of forthcoming steps (e.g., approval for large orders typically take longer than those for small orders).

Finally, we observe that this problem is more complicated than traditional processor scheduling or job shop scheduling problems, because the process structure also comes into play. Assume that our process has two parallel branches that synchronize at some point in the flow. There is no point in having one of the two advance fast if the other is progressing slowly. Hence, to order work items, we need to be aware of what is happening in the different branches of a process instance and make sure that all branches progress (or all branches do not progress, and we leave higher priority to other instances).

6 Time-Based Correlation

Another key problem in business process intelligence is that of relating metrics on the process to operational data such as the performance of IT resources that participate in the implementation of the process. This is important because it enables understanding of the *business impact* of operational problems.

Time-correlation algorithms can be used for automatic detection of time-dependent relationships among business metrics and operational data (e.g., the execution time of tasks in a process or performance of individual resources). In [Sayal05] the input to the algorithm is a set of numeric data streams, each of which contains the recorded numeric values of one variable (business metric or operational data variable) over the course of time. The output of the algorithm is a set of time-correlation rules that explain time-dependent relationships among data streams (numeric variables).

Detection of time-dependent relationships among hundreds or thousands of numeric variables is a difficult task that needs to be achieved in order to understand the cause-effect relationships among various events in a business. The method proposed in [Sayal05] transforms numeric data streams into sequences of discrete events that correspond to change points (or landmarks) in numeric values. This transformation reduces the search space of the algorithm by identifying the significant moments in time that can be used for summarizing the behavior of numeric variables. Then, the algorithm compares the change events from different data streams in order to detect co-occurrences of those events and calculate the statistical significance of the co-occurrences. The algorithm also calculates the typical time distance of the repeating co-occurrence patterns across data streams in order to generate time-correlation rules. Each time-correlation rule contains the following information:

- Numeric variables (data streams) that have time-dependent relationship
- Type of time-correlation (same or opposite direction)
- Sensitivity of time-correlation (how much the changes in one set of variables affect the values of another set of variables)
- Confidence (statistical confidence of the generated rule)

A typical time-correlation rule looks like the following:

A increases more than 5% → B decreases more than 10% within 2 days (conf: 85%)

The rule indicates a time-correlation between two variables, A and B, in the opposite direction such that the sensitivity of changes in B to the changes in A is high (approximately twice the amount of change in A), and the time duration to observe the impact of a change in A is two days. This information can be used for forecasting the behavior of business process instances, identifying the bottlenecks, and raising alerts in case certain thresholds are going to be exceeded based on the forecast values. As an example, the variables A and B might correspond to the performance of a particular resource and total execution time of a business process respectively. In that case, a business manager can be warned about deadlines that will be missed as a result of performance degradation in a particular resource.

7 Prediction and Proactive Optimization

Having visibility into the current state of business processes doesn't seem to suffice anymore. The ability to predict metrics and performance indicators gives the opportunity to proactively optimize the business process to improve its behavior (wrt its metrics). Predictions can be done at the instance level or at the aggregate level. The same applies to optimization. For example, we may want a prediction of the duration metric for a specific order of a customer to see if we will deliver the goods on time, and if not then we may want to increase the priority of the order so that it uses express shipment. We call this instance-based prediction (the prediction is done for a given instance while it is being executed) and dynamic optimization (the optimization is only for that instance and it is done during its execution), respectively. Instead, we may want to know if the average duration of orders on a certain day of next week will exceed the promised 24 hours delivery time (SLA violation) to plan for extra resources if needed. We call this type of prediction class-based time series prediction and static optimization is applied in this case.

While the first kind of prediction (i.e., instance-based) as its name suggests is based on the instance properties (e.g., day of the week that the order was submitted, type of product, region, etc), the second one is based on the time series of previous values of the metric. In consequence, suitable techniques for instance-based prediction belong to data mining, while a relaxed form of time series forecasting is used for the second one, [Castellanos05A].

In instance-based prediction [Grigori04] a model is generated from patterns mined from execution and business data associated to process instances. For example, a pattern may indicate that if an order was received on a Friday afternoon and step *check inventory* is performed by server S3, there is an 85% chance that the order won't get shipped in less than 24 hours. One of the main challenges for instance-based prediction is related to the fact that as a process instance makes progress in its execution its predictions need to be updated with the additional execution data that becomes available. The more the data, the more confidence there is in the prediction but at the same time the less time there is in taking action to prevent that a prediction (of an undesirable value) occurs. This means that different prediction models need to be built for different execution stages of a process. Since some processes have hundreds of steps, it doesn't make sense to have a prediction model after each step. Not only it is very costly to generate so many models, but it is useless to apply a model to each instance after the execution of each step since predictions will only change after some steps. The challenge is to find the execution stages that are relevant for prediction (i.e., prediction stages).

Class-based time series prediction [Castellanos05A] is a relaxed form of time series forecasting which takes advantage of the fact that extreme accuracy is not required when the goal is to predict whether a given metric will exceed a certain threshold or not, is within some specified range or not, or belongs to which one of a small number of specified classes. This gives the opportunity to completely automate the forecasting process to enable the analysis of hundreds or even thousands or business process metric time series. The main idea is to characterize a time series according to its components (i.e., trend and seasonality) and then apply the most appropriate technique(s) to create a good forecasting model [Castellanos05B]. Once the model is created it can be applied to obtain a numeric prediction which is mapped to the corresponding class (e.g., exceeds-threshold or not, within-range or not, low/medium/high). The main challenge, common to the instance-based models too, is how to quickly detect when the model is not good anymore and how to update it without having to rebuild it from scratch.

Once a prediction is obtained, different actions can be taken to optimize the process to improve the predicted value. When the prediction is made for a specific instance, it is possible to dynamically change things that only affect that instance to improve its execution. Typical actions are to assign a specific resource for a given action, change the priority of the instance, or dynamically change a selected path. In contrast, when the prediction is made for an aggregated metric, the optimization is static in the sense that it changes aspects of the process that are common to all its instances, like the number of resources of a given type that are allocated to a process.

Prediction opens up the opportunity to proactively optimize aspects of a process upon the alert of undesired predicted values. However, research is needed to maximize the potential for optimization. In particular, techniques for other kinds of optimization, including structural optimization where the order of the activities is changed and concurrency of activities is maximized. Also, techniques to identify what aspect(s) of a process execution are the most suitable to modify on the fly.

8 Conclusions

The transformation of the enterprise in response to business and technological changes has led to the concept of intelligent enterprise where business process intelligence is crucial to manage (monitoring, analyzing, and optimizing) the complexity of its inter- and intra-business processes. In this paper we have identified and briefly discussed challenges in business process intelligence. A prototype (Business Cockpit) that includes many of the capabilities described in this paper has been developed at HP Labs.

References

[Aalst03]	Wil van der Aalst, B.F. van Dongen, J. Herbst, L.Maruster, G.Schimm, A.J.M.M.Weijters. Workflow Mining: A Survey of Issues and Approachea. *Data and Knowledge Engineering, 47(2)*, 2003.
[Bonifati01]	Angela Bonifati, Fabio Casati, Umesh Dayal, and Ming-Chien Shan. Warehousing Workflow Data: Challenges and Opportunities. *Proceedings of VLDB01*, Rome, Italy. September 2001.
[Casati02]	Fabio Casati, Malu Castellanos, Umesh Dayal, Ming Hao, Ming-Chien Shan, Mehmet Sayal. Business Operation Intelligence Research at HP Labs. *Data Engineering Bulletin 25(4)*, December 2002.
[Casati04]	Fabio Casati, Malu Castellanos, Umesh Dayal, Ming-Chien Shan. Probabilistic, Context-Sensitive, and Goal-Oriented Service Selection. *Procs.oOf ICSOC'05*. New York, Nov 2004.
[Castellanos05A]	Malu Castellanos, Norman Salazar, Fabio Casati, Umesh Dayal, Ming-Chien Shan. Predictive Business Operations Management. *Procs. of DNIS'05*, Springer Verlag, May 2005.
[Castellanos05B]	Malu Castellanos, Norman Salazar, Fabio Casati, Ming-Chien Shan, Umesh Dayal. Automatic Metric Forecasting for Management Software. *Procs. OVUA Workshop*, Porto, Portugal, July 2005.
[Castellanos05C]	Malu Castellanos, Fabio Casati, Umesh Dayal, Ming-Chien Shan. iBOM: A Platform for Business Operation Management. Procs of ICDE 2005. Tokyo, Japan. Jun 2005.
[Grigori04]	Daniela Grigori, Fabio Casati, Malu Castellanos, Umesh Dayal, Ming-Chien Shan, Mehmet Sayal. Business Process Intelligence. *Computers in Industry* 53 (3). April *2004.*
[Rozinat05]	Ana Rozinat, Wil Van der Aalst. Conformance Testing: Measureing the Fit and Appropriateness of Event Logs and Process Models. *Procs. of BPI'05*, Nancy, France, September 2005.
[Sayal05]	Mehmet Sayal, Ming-Chien Shan. Analysis of Numeric Data Streams at Different Granularities. *IEEE International Conference on Granular Computing*. Beijing, China, July 2005.

Bootstrapping Domain Ontology for
Semantic Web Services from Source Web Sites

Wensheng Wu[1], AnHai Doan[1], Clement Yu[2], and Weiyi Meng[3]

[1] University of Illinois, Urbana, USA
[2] University of Illinois, Chicago, USA
[3] Binghamton University, Binghamton, USA

Abstract. The vision of Semantic Web services promises a network of interoperable Web services over different sources. A major challenge to the realization of this vision is the lack of automated means of acquiring domain ontologies necessary for marking up the Web services. In this paper, we propose the DeepMiner system which learns domain ontologies from the source Web sites. Given a set of sources in a domain of interest, DeepMiner first learns a base ontology from their query interfaces. It then grows the current ontology by probing the sources and discovering additional concepts and instances from the data pages retrieved from the sources. We have evaluated DeepMiner in several real-world domains. Preliminary results indicate that DeepMiner discovers concepts and instances with high accuracy.

1 Introduction

Past few years have seen an increasingly widespread deployment of Web services in the e-commerce marketplace such as travel reservation, book selling, and car sale services [21]. Among the most prominent contributing factors are several XML-based standards, such as WSDL [26], SOAP [20], and UDDI [22], which greatly facilitate the specification, invocation, and discovery of Web services. Nevertheless, the interoperability of Web services remains a grand challenge.

A key issue in enabling automatic interoperation among Web services is to *semantically* mark up the services with shared ontologies. These ontologies typically fall into two categories: service ontology and domain ontology. The *service ontology* provides generic framework and language constructs for describing the modeling aspects of Web services, including process management, complex service composition, and security enforcement. Some well-known efforts are OWL-S [5], WSFL [11], and WSMF [9]. The *domain ontology* describes concepts and concept relationships in the application domain, and facilitate the semantic markups on the domain-specific aspects of Web services such as service categories, semantic types of parameters, etc. Clearly, such semantic markups are crucial to the interoperation of the Web services.

Automatic acquisition of domain ontologies is a well-known challenging problem. To address this challenge, this paper proposes DeepMiner, a system for an incremental learning of domain ontologies for semantically marking up the Web

C. Bussler and M.-C. Shan (Eds.): TES 2005, LNCS 3811, pp. 11–22, 2006.

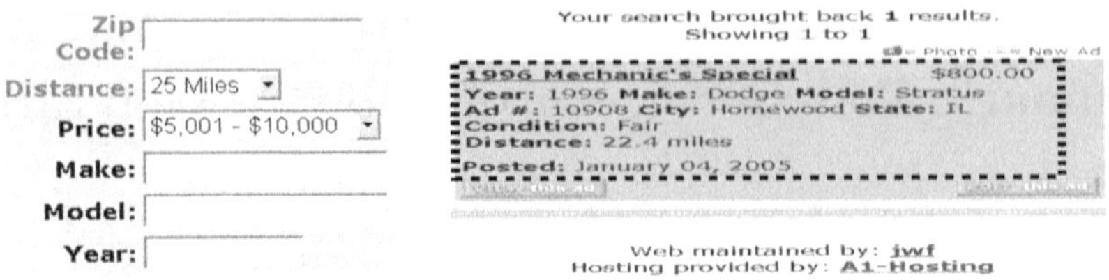

(a) Its query interface   (b) A snippet of a data page

Fig. 1. A car sale Web site: query interface and data page

services. DeepMiner is motivated by the following observations. First, we observe that many sources, which may potentially provide Web services, typically have already been providing similar services in their Web sites through query interface (e.g. in HTML form) and Web browser support. To illustrate, consider buying a car through a dealership's Web site. The purchasing may be conducted by first specifying some information on the desired vehicle such as make, model, and pricing, on its query interface (Figure 1.a). Next, the source may respond with the search result, i.e., a list of *data pages* (e.g., Figure 1.b), which typically contain detailed information on the qualified vehicles. The user may then browse the search result and place the order on the selected vehicle (e.g. through another HTML form).

Second, we observe that query interfaces and data pages of the sources often contain rich information on concepts, instances, and concept relationships in the application domain. For example, there are six attributes in Figure 1.a, each is denoted with a label and corresponds to a different concept. Some attributes may also have instances, e.g., Distance has instances such as 25 Miles. Further, the data page in Figure 1.b contains many additional concepts such as City, State, Condition, etc., and instances such as Homewood for City and Fair for Condition. Finally, the relative placement of attributes in the interface and data pages indicates their relationships, e.g., closely related attributes, such as Make and Model (both describe the vehicle), Zip Code and Distance (both concern the location of the dealership), are typically placed near to each other.

Based on the above observations, the goal of DeepMiner is to effectively learn a domain ontology from interfaces and data pages of a set of domain sources. Achieving this goal requires DeepMiner to make several innovations.

- **Incremental learning:** As observed above, the knowledge acquired from source interfaces only is often incomplete since data pages of the sources may contain many additional information. Further, different sources may contain a different set of concepts and instances. As such, DeepMiner learns the domain ontology in a snowballing fashion: first, it learns a base ontology from source interfaces; it then grows the current ontology by probing the sources and learning additional concepts and instances from the data pages retrieved from the sources.

- **Handling heterogeneities among sources:** Due to the autonomous nature of sources, the same concept may be represented quite differently over different sources. Another major challenge is thus to identify the semantic correspondences between concepts learned from different sources. To address this challenge, DeepMiner employs a clustering algorithm to effectively discover unique concepts over different interfaces. The learned ontology is then exploited for discovering new concepts and instances from data pages.

– **Knowledge-driven extraction:** Extracting concepts and instances from data pages is significantly more challenging than from query interfaces (since concepts and instances on an interface are typically enclosed in a form construct). To address this challenge, DeepMiner first exploits the current ontology to train concept classifiers. The concept classifiers are then employed to effectively identify regions of a data page where concepts and instances are located, discover presentation patterns, and perform the extraction.

The rest of the paper is organized as follows. Section 2 reviews related work. Section 3 defines the problem. Sections 4–5 describe the DeepMiner system. Empirical evaluation is reported in Section 6. Section 7 discusses the limitations of the current system. Section 8 concludes the paper.

2   Related Work

The problem of semantically marking up Web services is fundamental to the automated discovery and interoperation of Web services and e-services. As such, it is being actively researched [3, 4, 7, 8, 12, 14, 19, 23, 24].

There have been some efforts in learning domain ontology for Web services. Our work is most closely related to [17], but different in several aspects. First, [17] learns domain ontology from the documentations which might accompany the descriptions of Web services, while our work exploits the information from the source Web sites. Second, we extract concepts and instances from semi-structured data over source interfaces and data pages, while [17] learns ontology from natural language texts.

[15] proposes METEOR_S, a framework for annotating WSDL files with concepts from an existing domain ontology. The mappings between elements in the WSDL files and the concepts in the ontology are identified by exploiting a suite of matchers such as token matcher, synonym finder, and n-gram matcher. [10] employs several machine learning algorithms for the semantic annotation of attributes in source interfaces. The annotation relies on a manually constructed domain ontology. Our work is complementary to these works in that we aim to automatically learn a domain ontology from the information on the source Web sites. The learned ontology can then be utilized to annotate the Web services.

There are several previous work on extracting instances and their labels from data pages [1, 25]. A *fundamental* difference between these work and ours is that we utilize existing knowledge in the growing ontology to effectively identify data regions and occurrences of instances and labels on the data pages. We believe that such a *semantics-driven* approach is also more efficient than their template-induction algorithm which can have an exponential complexity [6].

The problem of matching interface attributes has also been studied in the context of integrating *deep Web* sources (e.g., [27]). Our work extends these works in the sense that the learned domain ontology can be used to construct a global schema for the sources.

3   Problem Definition

We consider the problem of learning a domain ontology from a given set of sources in a domain of interest. The learned domain ontology should have the following components: (1) *concepts:* e.g. make, model, and class are concepts of the auto sale domain. (2) *instances of concept:* e.g. Honda and Ford are instances of the concept make. (3) *synonyms:* e.g. the concept make may also be denoted by brand, car manufacturer, etc. (4) *statistics:* i.e., how frequent each concept and its instances appear in the domain. (5) *data types:* of the concept instances, e.g., instances of price are monetary values while instances of year are four-digit numbers. (6) *concept relationships:* which include the grouping (e.g, make and model), precedence (e.g., make should be presented before model), as well as the taxonomic relationships between concepts.

In this paper, we describe DeepMiner with respect to learning components (1)–(5). The details on the approaches for learning concept relationships will be given in the full version of the paper.

4   The DeepMiner Architecture

The architecture of DeepMiner is shown in Figure 2. Given a set of sources, DeepMiner starts by learning a base ontology O from source interfaces (step a). Then, the ontology-growing cycle (steps b–f) is initiated. At each cycle, first the current ontology O is exploited to train a label classifier C^l and an instance classifier C^i (step b). Next, DeepMiner poses queries to a selected source through its interface (step c) and obtains a set of data pages from the source (step d). The learned classifiers C^l and C^i are then employed to identify data regions in the data pages, from which DeepMiner extracts the occurrences of concepts and their instances (step e). Finally, the obtained concepts and instances are merged with O, resulting in a new ontology O' for the next cycle (step f).

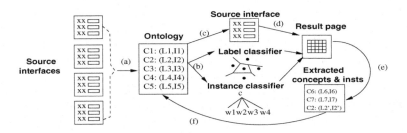

Fig. 2. The DeepMiner architecture

The rest of the section describes the process of learning base ontology. The details on the ontology-growing cycle will be presented in Section 5.

Consider a set of source query interfaces in a domain of interest (e.g. Figure 1.a). A query interface may be represented by a schema which contains a set of attributes. Each attribute may be associated with a label and a set of instances. The label and instances of attributes can be obtained from the interface by employing an automatic form extraction procedure [27].

Given a set of interfaces, DeepMiner learns a base ontology O which consists of all *unique* concepts and their instances over the interfaces. Since similar attributes (denoting the same concept) may be associated with different labels (e.g. Make of the car may be denoted as Brand on a different interface) and different sets of instances, a key challenge is thus to identify *semantic* correspondences (i.e. mappings) of different attributes over the interfaces.

For this, DeepMiner employs a single-link *clustering* algorithm [27] to effectively identify mappings of attributes over the interfaces. Specifically, the similarity of two attributes is evaluated based on the similarity of their labels (with the TF/IDF function commonly employed in Information Retrieval) and the similarity of the data type and values of their instances. (For the attributes with no instances, DeepMiner also attempts to glean their instances from the Web.) The data type of instances is *inferred* from the values of instances via pattern matching with a set of type-recognizing regular expressions. Finally, for each produced cluster, DeepMiner adds into its base ontology a new concept which contains the information obtained from the attributes in the cluster, including labels, instances, data type, and statistics as described in Section 3.

5   Growing Ontology Via Mining Data Pages

Denote the current ontology as O which contains a set of concepts, each of which is associated with a set of labels and instances. This section describes how DeepMiner grows O by mining additional concepts and instances from the data pages of a selected source. Query submission will be described in Section 6.

5.1   Training Label and Instance Classifiers

DeepMiner starts by training label classifier C^l and instance classifier C^i with training examples automatically created from O. C^l predicts the likelihood that a given string (of words) s may represent a concept in O, while C^i predicts the likelihood that a given string s' may be an instance of a concept in O.

Training Label Classifier: The label classifier C^l is a variant of the k-nearest neighbor (kNN) classifier [13], which performs the prediction by comparing the string with the concept labels it has seen during the training phase.

Specifically, at the training phase, for each concept $c \in O$ and each of its labels l, a training example (l, c) is created and stored with the classifier. Then, given a string s, C^l makes predictions on the class of s based on the classes of the stored examples whose similarity with s is larger than δ (i.e., the nearest neighbors of s), by taking votes. The similarity between two strings is their TF/IDF score [18].

Example 1. Suppose that O contains three concepts c_1, c_2, and c_3. Further suppose that the training examples stored with C^l are (l_1, c_1), (l_2, c_2), (l_3, c_3), (l_4, c_1), (l_5, c_2), and (l_6, c_3). Suppose that $\delta = .2$.

Consider a string s and suppose that the labels in the first five training examples (i.e., l_1 to l_5) are the ones whose similarity with s is greater than .2. Since $2/5$ of the nearest neighbors of s are from the concept c_1, the confidence score for c_1 is .4. The predictions for other concepts are given similarly.   □

Training Instance Classifier: The instance classifier C^i is a naive Bayes classifier which performs the prediction based on the frequency of words which occur in the instances of the concepts. Note that C^i may also be implemented as a kNN classifier, but since the number of instances of a concept is likely to be very large, the naive Bayes classifier is typically more efficient since it does not require the comparison with all the instances at the query time.

Specifically, for each instance i of a concept c in O, a training example (i', c) is created, where i' is a bag-of-token representation of i with the stopwords in i removed and the non-stop words stemmed. Then, given a string s, represented by $(w_1, w_2, \cdots, w_k)$, where w_i are tokens. C^i assigns, for each concept c in O, a prediction score $p(c|s)$ computed as $p(c) * p(s|c)/p(s)$, where $p(s)$ is $\sum_{c' in O} p(c') * p(s|c')$. Particularly, $p(c)$ is estimated as the percentage of training examples of class c. $p(s|c)$ is taken to be $p(w_1|c) * p(w_2|c) * \cdots * p(w_k|c)$, based on the assumption that tokens of s occur independently of each other given c. $p(w_i|c)$ is estimated as the ratio $n(w_i, c)/n(c)$, where $n(w_i, c)$ is the number of times token w_i appears in training examples whose class is the concept c, and $n(c)$ is the total number of token positions in all training examples of class c.

5.2   Mining Concepts and Instances

Identifying Data Regions: A data region is a portion of a data page which contains data records generated by the source, where each record consists of a set of instances and their labels. (Note that some instances may not have labels.) To illustrate, the data region in Figure 1.b is represented by a dashed box. Note that a data page may contain more than one data regions.

To identify the data regions, DeepMiner exploits the following observations. First, the current ontology O can be exploited to recognize data regions which may often contain labels and instances of existing concepts in O. Second, the label of a concept and its instances are often located in close proximity and spatially aligned on the data page [1]. This placement regularity can be exploited to associate the label of a concept with its instances.

Motivated by the above observations, DeepMiner starts by seeking the occurrences of concepts of O and their instances in the data page. Specifically, consider a data page p represented by its DOM tree. For example, Figure 3 shows the DOM tree for the data page in Figure 1.b. First, the label classifier C^l is employed to predict, for each text segment t (i.e. text node in the DOM tree), the

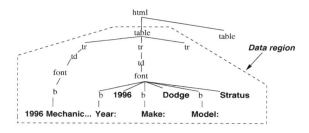

Fig. 3. The dom tree of Figure 1.b

concept c which t most likely denotes (i.e., c is the concept which C^l assigns the highest score s with $s > .5$). Next, t is further verified to see if it indeed denotes the concept c by checking if the text segment located below or next to t is an instance of c. Intuitively, these two positions are the places where instances of c are likely to be located.

To determine the relative position between two text segments, DeepMiner employs an approach which directly works on the DOM tree of the data page. The approach exploits the following observations on the characteristics of data pages. First, within each data region, the sequence of text segments resulted from a *pre-order* traversal of the DOM sub-tree for the data region often corresponds to the left-right, top-down ordering of text segments when the data page is rendered via Web browsers. Second, since data pages are automatically generated, spatial alignments of text segments are often achieved via the *table* construct of HTML, rather than via explicit white space characters such as " " which are often found in manually generated Web pages, e.g., with some Web page authoring tool. Based on these observations, DeepMiner takes the text segment which follows t in the pre-order traversal of the DOM tree to be the segment next to t, denoted as t_n. Further, if t is located in the cell $[i, j]$ of a table with M rows and N columns, then all text segments at column j and row k, where $i + 1 \leq k \leq N$, are taken to be the text segments *below* t, denoted as t_{b_k}'s.

Next, the instance classifier C^i is employed to determine, for each text segment t_x among t_n and t_{b_k}'s, the concept in O which t_x is most likely to be an instance of. Suppose t' has the largest confidence score among all these text segments and it is predicted to be an instance of class c'. Then, the text segment t is determined to denote the concept c only if $c' = c$. For example, State in Figure 1.b is recognized as a label for an existing concept c in O due to the fact that it is highly similar to some known label of c and further that IL (which is a text segment next to state) is predicted to be an instance of c by C^i.

The above procedure results in a set of label-instance pairs, each for some known concept in O. Data regions are then determined based on these label-instance pairs as follows. Consider such a label-instance pair, denoted as (L, I). If L is located in a table, then the data region induced by (L, I) comprises all content of the table. Otherwise, suppose the least-common-ancestor of nodes for L and I in the DOM tree is ω. The data region induced by (L, I) is then taken to be the subtree rooted at ω. The intuition is that related concepts are typically located near to each other in a data page and thus in the DOM tree of the data page as well.

Example 2. The DOM subtree which corresponds to the identified data region in Figure 1.b is marked with a dotted polygon in Figure 3.   □

Discovering Presentation Patterns: Once data regions are identified, DeepMiner proceeds to extract concepts and their instances from the data regions. For this, DeepMiner exploits a key observation that concepts and their instances within the same data region are typically presented in a similar fashion, to give an intuitive look-and-feel impression to users. For example, in Figure 1.b, the label of concept is shown in bold font and ends with a colon, and the corresponding instance is located right next to it, shown in normal font. Motivated by this observation, DeepMiner first exploits known concepts and their instances to discover their presentation patterns, and then applies the patterns to extract other concepts and their instances from the same data region.

Specifically, a presentation pattern for a concept label L and its instance I in a data region r is a 3-tuple: $<\alpha, \beta, \gamma>$, where α is the tag path to L from the root of the DOM subtree for r, β is the suffix of L (if any), and γ is the location of I relative to L. These patterns are induced from the known occurrences of label-instance pairs in the region r as follows. Denote the root of the DOM subtree for r as ω. For each label-instance pair (L_x, I_x), we induce a pattern. First, α is taken to be the sequence of HTML tags from ω to the text segment node for L_x, ignoring all hyperlink tags (i.e., 'a'). Second, if the text segment for L_x ends with symbols such as ':', '-' and '/', these symbols constitute β. Third, γ has two possible values: *next* and *below*, depending on how I_x is located, relative to L_x.

Example 3. α for the data region in Figure 3 is (table, tr, td, font, b), β is the suffix ':', and the value of γ is *next*.   □

Extracting Concept Labels and Instances: This step employs the learned patterns to extract concept labels and their instances from the data region r. In particular, α and β of a pattern are first applied to identify labels of other concepts in the region and then the instances of the identified concepts are extracted in the location relative to the labels as indicated by the γ part of the pattern.

Example 4. The learned pattern from Figure 3 will extract concept-instances pairs from Figure 1.b such as: (Year, {1996}), (Make, {Dodge}), and (Posted, {January 04, 2005}).   □

5.3   Merging with the Current Ontology

This step merges the label-instances pairs mined from the data pages into the current ontology O. Specifically, for each label-instances pair $e = (L, I)$, if e belongs to an existing concept c, then L and I are added to the list of labels and instances for c, respectively. The corresponding statistics for c are also updated accordingly. Otherwise, a new concept will be created with L as a label and I as a set of instances.

6   Empirical Evaluation

We have conducted preliminary experiments to evaluate DeepMiner. The experiments use an e-commerce data set which contains sources over automobile, book and job domains, with 20 sources in each domain [2]. Each source has a query interface represented by a set of attributes. The average number of attributes for the interfaces in the auto, book and job domains is 5.1, 5.4, and 4.6, respectively.

First, we evaluated the performance of DeepMiner on discovering unique concepts over source interfaces. The performance is measured by two metrics: *precision*, which is the percentage of correct mappings of attributes among all the mappings identified by the system, and *recall*, which is the percentage of correct mappings among all mappings given by domain experts. In these experiments, the clustering threshold is set to .25, uniformly over all domains. Results are shown in columns 2–3 in Table 1.

Table 1. The performance of DeepMiner

Domains	Base Ontology		Data Regions		Concept-Instances	
	Prec.	Rec.	Prec.	Rec.	Prec.	Rec.
Auto	100	98.9	6/7	6/6	41/43	41/41
Book	100	90.4	8/8	8/8	41/41	41/43
Job	94.6	91.2	5/5	5/5	22/22	22/23

It can be observed that attribute mappings are identified with high precision over all domains, with a prefect precision in the auto and book domains and around 95% for the job domain. Furthermore, good recalls are also achieved, ranging from 90.4% in the book domain to 98.9% in the auto domain. Detailed analysis indicates the challenge of matching some attributes in the book domain, e.g., DeepMiner failed to match attributes section and category since their instances have very little in common. A possible remedy is to utilize the instances obtained from data pages to help identify their mapping.

To isolate the effects of different components, we manually examined the mapping results and corrected mismatches. This process takes only a couple of minutes, since there are very few errors in each domain.

Next, we evaluated the performance of DeepMiner on identifying data regions. For this, we randomly select five sources for each domain. For each source, query submission is made by automatically formulating a query string which consists of form element names and values, and posing the query to the source. If an attribute does not have instances in its interface, the instances of its similar attributes (available from the base ontology) are used instead. This probing process is repeated until at least one valid data page is returned from the source, judged based on several heuristics as employed in [16]. For example, pages which contain phrases such as "no results" and "no matches" are regarded as invalid pages.

For all data pages retrieved in each domain, we first manually identified the number of data regions in the pages, and use it as the gold standard. Deep-Miner's performance is then measured by the number of data regions it *correctly* identified, over all data regions it identified (i.e. precision), and over all the expected data regions as given by the gold standard (i.e. recall). Results are shown in columns 4–5 of Table 1. It can observed that DeepMiner is very accurate in identifying data regions: only one is incorrectly identified in the auto domain.

Finally, we evaluated DeepMiner's performance on discovering concepts and their instances from data pages. This was done by first manually determining the number of concept labels and their instances in all data pages, and then comparing the concept-instances pairs discovered by DeepMiner with this gold standard. Results are shown in the last two columns of Table 1.

We observe that DeepMiner achieves very high accuracy consistently over different domains. We looked at the data pages it made mistakes and examined the reasons. In particular, we note that there is a concept with label job description: in www.aftercollege.com, but its instance is located in the same text segment as the label, although the label does contain a delimiter ':'. It would be interesting to extend DeepMiner to handle such cases. DeepMiner also made some errors in Amazon.com. For example, currently it is difficult for DeepMiner to recognize that only Prentice Hall in Prentice Hall (feb 8, 2008) is an instance of publisher. We are currently developing a solution which exploits the existing ontology to perform *segmentation* on the text segments.

7   Discussions and Future Work

We now address the limitations of the current DeepMiner system. The first issue to address is to make the learning of presentation patterns more robust, e.g., handling possible non-table constructs. Currently, the relative positions of attributes and their values are obtained by analyzing their appearance in the DOM trees. An alternative is to render the data page with a Web browser and obtain the spatial relationships (e.g., pixel distances and alignments) of attributes and values from the rendered page. But this approach has a potential disadvantage of being time-consuming.

Second, we plan to perform additional experiments with the system and further examine its performance. Preliminary results indicated that data pages are typically rich in attributes and values, and that a dozen of data pages per Web site are often sufficient for learning a sizable ontology. As such, we expect our approach to be scalable to a large number of Web sites.

Finally, it would be interesting to combine our approach with the approaches of learning concepts and instances from the Web services already existing in the B2B domain (e.g. [17]). Further, the ontology learned with our approach can be utilized to train concept and instance classifiers, which can then be employed to markup the Web services by the approaches such as [15].

8   Conclusions

We have described the DeepMiner system for learning domain ontology from the source Web sites. The learned ontology can then be exploited to mark up Web services. Its key novelties are (1) incremental learning of concepts and instances; (2) effective handling of the heterogeneities among autonomous sources; and (3) a machine learning framework which exploits existing ontology in the process of learning new concepts and instances. Preliminary results indicated that it discovers concepts and instances with high accuracy.

We are currently investigating several directions to extend DeepMiner: (a) employ the learned ontology to segment complex text segments and recognize instances in the segments; (b) utilize the instances gleaned from data pages to assist in matching interface attributes; and (c) combine DeepMiner with the approach of learning domain ontology from texts.

Acknowledgment. This research is supported in part by the following grants from NSF: IIS-0414981 and IIS-0414939.

References

1. L. Arlotta, V. Crescenzi, G. Mecca, and P. Merialdo. Automatic annotation of data extracted from large Web sites. In *WebDB*, 2003.
2. http://metaquerier.cs.uiuc.edu/repository/.
3. B. Benatallah, M. Hacid, A. Leger, C. Rey, and F. Toumani. On automating web services discovery. *VLDB Journal*, 14(1), 2005.
4. F. Casati and M. Shan. Models and languages for describing and discovering e-services. In *Tutorial, SIGMOD*, 2001.
5. The OWL-S Services Coalition. OWL-S: Semantic Markup for Web Services. http://www.w3.org/Submission/OWL-S/.
6. V. Crescenzi, G. Mecca, and P. Merialdo. RoadRunner: Towards automatic data extraction from large Web sites. In *Proc. of VLDB*, 2001.
7. G. Denker, L. Kagal, T. Finin, M. Paolucci, and K. Sycara. Security for daml web services: Annotation and matchmaking. In *ISWC*, 2003.
8. M. Dumas, J. O'Sullivan, M. Hervizadeh, D. Edmond, and A. Hofstede. Towards a semantic framework for service description. In *DS-9*, 2001.
9. D. Fensel and C. Bussler. The Web Service Modeling Framework WSMF. *Electronic Commerce: Research and Applications*, 1, 2002.
10. A. Heß and N. Kushmerick. Machine learning for annotating semantic web services. In *AAAI Spring Symposium on Semantic Web Services*, 2004.
11. F. Leymann. WSFL (Web Service Flow Language), 2001.
12. B. Li, W. Tsai, and L. Zhang. Building e-commerce systems using semantic application framework. *Int. J. Web Eng. Technol.*, 1(3), 2004.
13. T. Mitchell. *Machine Learning*. McGraw-Hill, 1997.
14. M. Paolucci and K. Sycara. Semantic web services: Current status and future directions. In *ICWS*, 2004.
15. A. Patil, S. Oundhakar, A. Sheth, and K. Verma. METEOR-S: Web service annotation framework. In *WWW*, 2004.
16. S. Raghavan and H. Garcia-Molina. Crawling the hidden Web. In *VLDB*, 2001.
17. M. Sabou, C. Wroe, C. Goble, and G. Mishne. Learning domain ontologies for web service descriptions: an experiment in bioinformatics. In *WWW*, 2005.
18. G. Salton and M. McGill. *Introduction to Modern Information Retrieval*. McCraw-Hill, New York, 1983.

19. K. Sivashanmugam, K. Verma, A. Sheth, and J. Miller. Adding semantics to web services standards. In *ICWS*, 2003.
20. SOAP. http://www.w3.org/TR/soap/.
21. http://uddi.microsoft.com/.
22. UDDI. http://www.uddi.org/.
23. D. VanderMeer, A. Datta, et al. FUSION: A system allowing dynamic Web service composition and automatic execution. In *CEC*, 2003.
24. L. Vasiliu, M. Zaremba, et al. Web-service semantic enabled implementation of machine vs. machine business negotiation. In *ICWS*, 2004.
25. J. Wang and F. Lochovsky. Data extraction and label assignment for Web databases. In *WWW*, 2003.
26. WSDL. http://www.w3.org/TR/wsdl/.
27. W. Wu, C. Yu, A. Doan, and W. Meng. An interactive clustering-based approach to integrating source query interfaces on the Deep Web. In *SIGMOD*, 2004.

Systematic Design of Web Service Transactions

Benjamin A. Schmit and Schahram Dustdar

Vienna University of Technology, Information Systems Institute,
Distributed Systems Group, Vienna, Austria, Europe
{benjamin, dustdar}@infosys.tuwien.ac.at

Abstract. The development of composite Web services is still not as simple as the original vision indicated. Currently, the designer of a composite service needs to consider many different design aspects at once. In this paper, we propose a modeling methodology based on UML which separates between the four concerns of structure, transactions, workflow, and security, each of which can be modeled by different experts. We have developed a proof-of-concept tool that is able to extract information from the model and transform it into a computer-readable format.

1 Introduction

Web services have become more and more commonplace during the last few years. An idea that has been associated with them from the start is that of composition: Web services should be located at run-time and assembled semi-automatically to provide more complex services. This goal, however, still involves some unsolved research questions, among others in the field of distributed long-running transactions.

An important aspect of Web service composition is that the designer or maintainer of a composite service until now had to be an expert in several fields. We have identified a need for knowledge about Web service structure (which services are used by which composite services), transactional issues, security issues, and about the workflow of the composite service. We therefore propose to split composite Web service design into these four views. Four largely independent models can then be created by different experts, with connections between them only where it is necessary.

Minor updates to a composite service are also facilitated by our approach since only a subset of the design diagrams need to be changed. Software tools can further help the programmer by automating transformations from design diagrams to (preliminary) code. Therefore, we have based our methodlogy on the Unified Modeling Language (UML), which is already supported by most design tools.

The methodology has not yet been fully completed, but the models developed with it can already be used profitably. As a proof of concept, we have developed a transformation tool based on the widely used Eclipse platform which extracts transaction information from the model. The output conforms to the

C. Bussler and M.-C. Shan (Eds.): TES 2005, LNCS 3811, pp. 23–33, 2006.

WS-Coordination specification and could easily be incorporated into a Web service platform implementing this specification.

Section 2 introduces a composite Web service case study that will be used to illustrate our work. Section 3 presents the elements of our UML metamodel and applies this metamodel to the case study. Section 4 presents our modeling tool and shows how it can extract information from the model created from our case study. Section 5 presents related work, and Section 6 concludes the paper.

2   Case Study

In this section, we will introduce a case study which we will refer to throughout the paper. Instead of using the traditional composite Web service example of a travel reservation system, we refer to our case study first introduced in [1], which describes the production of a movie in terms of Web services. Modeling such a comprehensive example with Web services may involve unprecedented design decisions as well as unexpected outcomes. It should lead to a more realistic estimate of the benefits of our methodology.

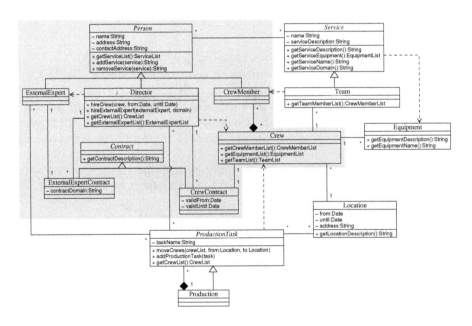

Fig. 1. Film production case study

Figure 1 shows an overview on the case study. Because of the space limitation, we will concentrate on how the director of the movie hires film crews for the production of the film and external experts who assist him with their expertise (depicted in grey in Figure 1). Both processes need to be handled within a transaction scope.

In our example, experts and crews provide Web services which may be looked up via a Web services registry. A software architect in the director's office composes these services into a new service, which is then used by the director.

3   The UML Metamodel

We will now introduce a uniform methodology for Web services modeling based on the Unified Modeling Language (UML, [2]). An overview on this methodology has first been presented in [3].

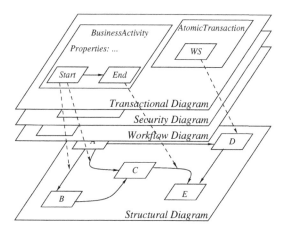

Fig. 2. A Design methodology for Web services

Figure 2 depicts the design idea. It is based on the paradigm of separation of concerns. The four concerns identified so far are structural, transactional, security, and workflow issues. (The order is different in the figure because we focus on the transactional diagram.) Each concern can be modeled by an independent expert, and the Object Constraint Language (OCL; part of the UML specification) is used to establish references between the diagrams.

As we have demonstrated in [3], using separate diagrams for separate design aspects makes the model easier to read, and different experts can work on the design simultaneously. The obvious drawback of this separation, the higher complexity of the methodology, is kept as small as possible by using OCL references between the different layers. We believe that workflow and transaction aspects belong to separate layers because this eases later corrections (e.g., adjusting transaction quality of service parameters). On the other hand, a part of the workflow diagram may be referenced e.g. as a compensation handler.

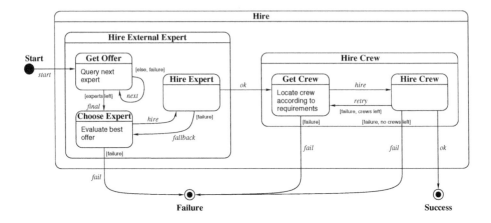

Fig. 3. Example structural diagram

3.1   The Structural Diagram

For the structural diagram, we have chosen a UML statechart diagram. The Unified Modeling Language [2] has been chosen because it is widely used for modeling software and fits our purposes. We chose a statechart diagram (instead of adding a new diagram type that might more closely describe Web service structure) because existing tools already support this diagram type. Since we have not yet specified the workflow diagram, some workflow details are still included in the structural diagram.

The semantics that have been added to the diagram for Web services modeling (guards and threads maintain their existing semantics) are shown in Table 1.

Figure 3 shows a structural diagram of our example. Elements (transitions) from this diagram will be referenced in the transactional diagram.

Table 1. Added semantics for the structural diagram

● →	**Start element.** Processing of the composite Web service starts here.
→ ◉	**End element.** Processing of the composite Web service terminates here. Annotations may be either *Success* or *Failure*, which indicate whether the composite service terminates normally or abnormally at that point.
→	**Transition.** Indicates that another task of a Web service is handled next, or that the Web service is started (from the start element) or terminated (to the end element).
Composite Task / Task / Description	**Task.** Composite tasks contain inner elements (tasks, transitions). Instead, non-composite tasks may contain a description (not intended to be processed).

3.2   The Transactional Diagram

The transactional view is formed by a UML class diagram. Again, we have chosen an existing UML diagram type so that existing UML tools do not need to be modified for processing the transactional diagram. We have used OCL references to identify the locations within the structural diagram where transactions are started, committed, or aborted. A UML profile describes the additional constraints for the transactional diagram.

In the diagram, a transaction is depicted as a UML class, i.e., as a box with three compartments. The first compartment contains the name of the transaction, a stereotype describing the transactional semantics, and tagged values that describe quality of service attributes. The second compartment names the participating Web services (the keyword *dynamic* indicates that the Web service is to be located at run-time, a process which is not covered by this paper). The third compartment holds the references to the start and end of the transaction, as well as invocations to other Web services (starting points for other transactions). Finally, the inheritance relationship is used to model subtransactions. Table 2 defines the keywords used within the UML profile for the transactional diagram.

Figure 4 shows an example of a transactional diagram. The three main transactions corresponding to the first two levels of states in Figure 3 are easily derived from the structural diagram. The start and termination transitions are indicated by OCL references, in the outermost transaction these are *Start.start*, *HireCrew.ok*, *ChooseExpert.fail*, *GetCrew.fail*, and *HireCrew.fail*. They

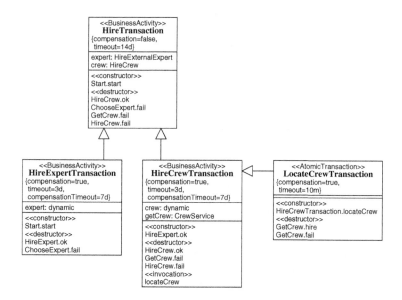

Fig. 4. Example transactional diagram

Table 2. Keywords in the transaction profile

Keyword	UML Scope	Description
Invocation	Class Stereotype	A Web service invocation running without a transactional scope, i.e. no transaction.
AtomicTransaction	Class Stereotype	An ACID transaction, as defined in [4].
BusinessActivity	Class Stereotype	A long-running, non-ACID transaction, as defined in [5].
compensation	Class Tagged Value	Flag that specifies whether the transaction as a whole can be compensated.
timeout	Class Tagged Value	Maximum time interval that the transaction can be active before it is rolled back.
compensationTimeout	Class Tagged Value	Maximum time interval measured from the start of a transaction that a committed transaction can be compensated.
dynamic	Attribute Type	Indicates that a Web service is to be bound at run-time.
constructor	Method Stereotype	Starting point for the transaction.
destructor	Method Stereotype	Termination point for the transaction.
invocation	Method Stereotype	Starting point for a subtransaction which is not depicted in the structural diagram.

correspond to the arrows entering and leaving the *Hire* state in the structural diagram.

Our example, however, also contains a fourth transaction that is used for finding film crews that may later be contacted to participate in the current production. Instead of referencing the structural diagram, the starting point of the *LocateCrewTransaction* lies within the *HireCrewTransaction*, i.e. within the transactional diagram itself. In the *HireCrewTransaction*, this starting point is described as a method stereotyped *invocation*.

3.3 Security and Workflow Issues

Since security aspects should be considered as early as possible, we propose the inclusion of security parameters (e.g., which Web service calls/transactions need to be encrypted or signed) in the design phase. We do not have developed a diagram for security yet. We intend to use OCL for references to entities in both the structural and the transactional design diagram, but this is still subject to future work.

The workflow diagram will offer a high-level view on the composite Web service. This design view will cover issues that cannot be addressed by the structural and transactional diagram alone, e.g. some of the challenges introduced in [3]. This diagram will reference elements of the structural and the transactional view.

4   Tool Support

In order to show the usefulness of our design approach, we have implemented a proof-of-concept tool that works on the transactional design diagram. It has been built on the Eclipse platform [6] extended by the IBM Rational Software Architect tool suite [7].

4.1   Architecture

Eclipse is a highly modular integrated development environment for Java which also offers basic support for the Unified Modeling Language (UML, [8]) through the Eclipse Modeling Framework (EMF, [9]).

The IBM Rational Software Architect extends this platform, among other things, by adding a visual editor for creating and maintaining UML models. Transformations allow the developer to automatically transform the model into a code skeleton and synchronize changes in design and code. Transformations for creating Java, EJB, and C++ code are included.

We have written an extension to this platform which adds a new transformation method to the modeler. It extracts the transactions from a UML class diagram following the specification of our transactional diagram. The output currently consists of a coordination context for use in WS-Coordination, WS-AtomicTransaction, and WS-BusinessActivity [10, 4, 5], however, it can easily be adapted to confirm to other transaction specifications.

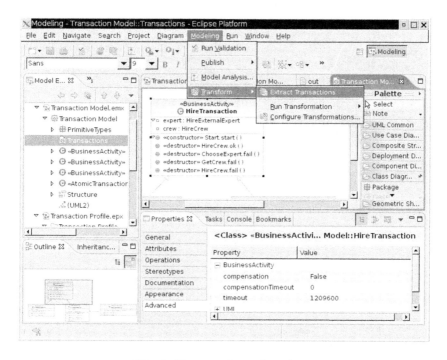

Fig. 5. The transformation plugin

4.2   Application to the Case Study

Figure 5 shows the transactional diagram on which the transformation is invoked in the so-called modeling perspective. The modeling perspective consists of four windows:

The model explorer (top left) shows a tree view of the elements within the project. In the example, we see the model with two diagrams and the *Transaction Profile* which defines the stereotypes used in the transactional diagram. The outline window (bottom left) shows a bird-eye view on the current diagram.

In the main window (top right), a part of the transactional design diagram can be seen. The class *HireTransaction* has been selected.

In the bottom right window, properties of the selected transaction can be seen. Within the EMF, they have been modeled as attributes to the *Business-Activity* stereotype of the *Transaction Profile* UML profile. This helps to keep the diagram lean (because such attributes are per default not shown in the main window), but still allows for a simple extraction by our plugin.

Figure 6 shows a simple output XML file the transformation plugin has generated from a part of our design. Right now, only the transactional model is considered by the prototype tool, but already its output could be used as a coordination context in a WS-BusinessActivity transaction. Changes in the design lead to changes in the context, taking some of the load away from the programmer of the composite Web service.

Fig. 6. Output of the transformation plugin

4.3   Outlook

In the future, we plan to extend the tool so that it allows more comprehensive modeling and also considers the structural view. We aim to be able finally to extract a process description in BPEL [11] and/or a choreography description in WS-CDL [12] from our model, thereby greatly easing the task of Web service composition. Using the information contained in the design diagrams, these descriptions can be enriched by using various additional Web service related specifications.

When this work has been completed, we will explore the potential for further automation through the use of a security and a workflow diagram.

5   Related Work

Several independent (sets of) Web service transaction specifications have been released: WS-Coordination, WS-AtomicTransaction, and WS-BusinessActivity [10, 4, 5] have been used for the implementation of our tool. Possible alternatives would have been WS-CAF ([13], consisting of WS-Context, WS-Coordination Framework, and WS-Transaction Management) or BTP [14].

Orriëns, Yang, and Papazoglou [15] divide the process of Web service composition into four phases: definition, scheduling, construction, and execution. The design should become more concrete at each step. UML is used as well, however, the model is founded on the design process and not on separation of concerns.

Dijkman and Dumas [16] also state the need for a multi-viewpoint design approach for composite Web services. Their paper discusses the views of interface behavior, provider behavior, choreography, and orchestration and uses Petri nets for the model itself. Distributed transactions are not mentioned.

Benatallah, Dumas, and Sheng [17] also use statechart diagrams to model composite Web services. Transactional behavior is mentioned as future work, but as yet there is no systematic approach for modeling this.

Karastoyanova and Buchmann [18] propose a template technique for Web services to ease service composition. Templates here are parts of a business process description that can be used for Web service composition. The concept may prove useful for transforming our model diagrams into business process specifications in the future.

Loecher [19] discusses properties of transactions in a distributed middleware setting. Though the author writes about Enterprise JavaBeans, some of the work can be applied to Web services as well.

Henkel, Zdravkovic, and Johannesson [20] mention the difference between technical and business requirements. Their paper proposes a layered architecture that allows to transform the business representation into a more technical representation. Several aspects of process design are described, among them also a transactional aspect.

Jablonski, Böhm, and Schulze [21] propose a separation of concern approach for workflow modeling called workflow aspects. They distinguish between a functional, a behavioral, an informational, an operational, and an organizational aspect. The book surveys workflow modeling and also mentions transaction and security issues.

Further information about Web service transaction specifications can be found in [22]. Database transactions are covered by [23], and additional information about advanced transaction models can be found in [24, 25].

6   Conclusion

In this paper, we have introduced a modeling methodology for composite Web services based on UML. The methodology is based on the concept of separation of concern, i.e., several experts can work on different aspects of the design concurrently. We have defined the structural and the transactional diagram and outlined our future work on the workflow and security diagrams.

We have shown the usefulness of our approach by implementing a transformation tool based on the Eclipse platform. This tool extracts transaction information from the model and transforms this information into a machine-readable XML document following the WS-Coordination specification.

The next steps in our research will be the development and formalization of the workflow and security diagrams. Also, we will expand our transformation tool towards a more comprehensive view on the model. Hereby, we hope to be able to automatically generate more complex descriptions, e.g., a BPEL or WS-CDL description. This automation will help designers to considerably simplify the development of composite Web services.

References

1. Schmit, B.A., Dustdar, S.: Towards transactional web services. In: Proceedings of the 1st IEEE International Workshop on Service-oriented Solutions for Cooperative Organizations (SoS4CO'05), 7th International IEEE Conference on E-Commerce Technology, Munich, Germany, IEEE (2005) To be published.
2. OMG: The unified modeling language, version 2.0. Specification (2004)
3. Schmit, B.A., Dustdar, S.: Model-driven development of web service transactions. In: Proceedings of the 2nd GI-Workshop XML for Business Process Management, 11. GI-Fachtagung für Datenbanksysteme in Business, Technologie und Web, Karlsruhe, Germany, Gesellschaft für Informatik (2005) To be published.
4. BEA, IBM, Microsoft: Web services atomic transaction (WS-AtomicTransaction). Specification (2004)
5. BEA, IBM, Microsoft: Web services business activity framework (WS-BusinessActivity). Specification (2004)
6. Beck, K., Gamma, E.: Contributing to Eclipse. Principles, Patterns, and Plug-Ins. Addison-Wesley (2003)
7. Lau, C., Yu, C., Fung, J., Popescu, V., McKay, E., Flood, G., Mendel, G., Winchester, J., Walker, P., Deboer, T., Lu, Y.: An Introduction to IBM Rational Application Developer: A Guided Tour. IBM Press (2005) To be published.
8. Rumbaugh, J., Jacobson, I., Booch, G.: The Unified Modeling Language Reference Manual. 2nd edn. Addison-Wesley (2004)

9. Budinsky, F., Steinberg, D., Merks, E., Ellersick, R., Grose, T.J.: Eclipse Modeling Framework. Addison-Wesley (2003)
10. BEA, IBM, Microsoft: Web services coordination (WS-Coordination). Specification (2004)
11. BEA, IBM, Microsoft, SAP, Siebel: Business process execution language for web services (BPEL4WS), version 1.1. Specification (2003) Adopted by OASIS as WS-BPEL.
12. Oracle, Commerce One, Novell, Choreology, W3C: Web services choreography description language version 1.0, W3C working draft 17 december 2004. Specification (2004)
13. Arjuna, Fujitsu, IONA, Oracle, Sun: Web services composite application framework (WS-CAF). Specification (2003)
14. OASIS: Business transaction protocol, version 1.1.0. Specification (2004)
15. Orriëns, B., Yang, J., Papazoglou, M.P.: Model driven service composition. In: Proceedings of the First International Conference on Service Oriented Computing. Volume 2910 of Lecture Notes in Computer Science., Springer-Verlag (2003) 75–90
16. Dijkman, R., Dumas, M.: Service-oriented design: A multi-viewpoint approach. International Journal of Cooperative Information Systems **13** (2004) 337–368
17. Benatallah, B., Dumas, M., Sheng, Q.Z.: Facilitating the rapid development and scalable orchestration of composite web services. Distributed and Parallel Databases **17** (2005) 5–37
18. Karastoyanova, D., Buchmann, A.: Automating the development of web service compositions using templates. In: Proceedings of the Workshop "Geschäftsprozessorientierte Architekturen" at Informatik 2004, Gesellschaft für Informatik (2004)
19. Loecher, S.: A common basis for analyzing transaction service configurations. In: Proceedings of the Software Engineering and Middleware Workshop 2004. Lecture Notes in Computer Science, Springer-Verlag (2004) To be published.
20. Henkel, M., Zdravkovic, J., Johannesson, P.: Service-based processes — design for business and technology. In: Proceedings of the Second International Conference on Service Oriented Computing. (2004) 21–29
21. Jablonski, S., Böhm, M., Schulze, W.: Workflow-Management: Entwicklung von Anwendungen und Systemen. Dpunkt Verlag (1997)
22. Papazoglou, M.P.: Web services and business transactions. World Wide Web **6** (2003) 49–91
23. Gray, J., Reuter, A.: Transaction Processing: Concepts and Techniques. Morgan Kaufmann Series in Data Management Systems. Morgan Kaufmann (1993)
24. Elmagarmid, A.K., ed.: Database Transaction Models for Advanced Applications. Morgan Kaufmann Series in Data Management Systems. Morgan Kaufmann (1992)
25. Procházka, M.: Advanced Transactions in Component-Based Software Architectures. PhD thesis, Charles University Prague, Faculty of Mathematics and Physics, Department of Software Engineering (2002)

A Matching Algorithm for Electronic Data Interchange

Rami Rifaieh[1], Uddam Chukmol[2], and Nabila Benharkat[3]

[1] San Diego Supercomputer Center, University of California San Diego,
9500 Gilman Dr. La Jolla, CA 92093-0505, USA
rrifaieh@sdsc.edu
[2] Computer Science Department, Combodia Technological Institute,
P.O. Box 86, Bld. Pochentong, Phnom Penh, Cambodia
uddam.chukmol@itc.edu.kh
[3] LIRIS – National Institute of Applied Science of Lyon,
7 Avenue J.Capelle, 69621 Villeurbanne, France
nabila.benharkat@insa-lyon.fr

Abstract. One of the problems in the actual electronic commerce is laid on the data heterogeneity (i.e. format and vocabulary). This representation incompatibility, particularly in the EDI (Electronic Data Interchange), is managed manually with help from a human expert consulting the usage guideline of each message to translate. This manual work is tedious, error-prone and expensive. The goal of this work is to partially automate the semantic correspondence discovery between the EDI messages of various standards by using XML Schema as the pivot format. This semi-automatic schema matching algorithm take two schemata of EDI messages as the input, compute the basic similarity between each pair of elements by comparing their textual description and data type. Then, it computes the structural similarity value basing on the structural neighbors of each element (ancestor, sibling, immediate children and leaf elements) with an aggregation function. The basic similarity and structural similarity values are used in the pair wise element similarity computing which is the final similarity value between two elements. The paper shows as well some implementation issues and a scenario of test for EX-SMAL with messages coming from EDIFACT and SWIFT standards.

1 Introduction

Electronic Data Interchange (EDI) is characterized by the possibility of sending/treating messages between information systems without any human intervention. The emergence of EDI enables companies to communicate easily (e.g. Send Orders, Funds Transfer, Acknowledgement of receipt, etc.). With growing business, many companies have to treat different type of messages and standards. Therefore, a large number of translations are needed in order to enable the communication between an enterprise and its suppliers and clients [21].

Although the use of XML has simplified the task of data exchange, the problem of data heterogeneity remains largely unresolved [17]. For the same kind of data, independent developers and systems often use XML syntaxes (i.e. messages) that have very little in common. For example, a Payment Order schema can generate an XML document where the date of the payment order looks like:

C. Bussler and M.-C. Shan (Eds.): TES 2005, LNCS 3811, pp. 34–47, 2006.
© Springer-Verlag Berlin Heidelberg 2006

```
< PaymentOrder>
    <orderDate> 30/07/2004 </orderDate>
<PaymentOrder>
```

Whereas the encoding chosen by a partner defines the date of a payment order with:

```
< POrder>
    <Header>
        <POIssue Date = "30-07-04" />
    </Header>
</POrder>
```

These two documents contain the same data (date of payment order) but with two incompatible representation. Thus, establishing translation between different sources is a hard task without the presence of an expert which can identify the similarity between different elements of equivalent representations. In order to simplify this manual tedious and error-prone work, we suggest automating the similarity findings. We explore in this paper the development of an EDI/XML semi-automatic Schema Matching Algorithm. The algorithm uses XML Schema, as the pivot, to represent the schemas of EDI messages.

The paper is organized as follows. In the Section 2, we survey the literature for related works. We bring out the difficulties in existing approaches to suit EDI Schema matching. We present in Section 3 our similarity algorithm. We examine the used module and argue their usefulness. In section 4, we show some practical issues concerning implementation, scenario of test, and results. We wrap up our paper with future works and conclusion showing the assets, apportunities, and limits of our algorithm.

2 Related Works

In order to apply a translation between different representations, we should use two distinguished processes: matching and mapping. Firstly, matching process helps to identify the correspondent elements. Afterward a mapping process is required to express how the matched elements can be mapped. The input of the first is the schema or the branching diagram of the messages. The output is a list of matched elements. The input of the mapping process is the list of matched elements and the output is the individual mapping expression of target elements. We are only interested in this paper by the first process (i.e. similarity matching). Other works concerning mapping expression can be found in [22] and [18].

There is much literature on matching algorithms using learning module or thesaurus. These algorithms differentiate between being content based analysis (instance matching) XMapper [13], Automatch [2], and LSD [7], representation based analysis (schema matching) [12], [24], and [15], and usage based analysis (ontology matching) H-Match [5], Glue [8], and [3]. However, the algorithms with learning capabilities have a handicap concerning the needed training. Using thesaurus for improving the matching process is very interesting where schema's elements have linguistically representative names. In all these approaches, we are only interested by representation based analysis since EDI branching diagrams, i.e. usage guide, are very likely to schemas.

Table 1. Functional comparison

	COMA	Cupid	Similarity Flooding
Schema Type	Relational, XML Schema	Relational XML Schema	XML Schema, RDF, UML et OEM SQL DDL,
Internal Data structure	Acyclic oriented graph	Acyclic oriented graph	OIM format labeled graph
Human intervention	Possible	Specifying domain vocabulary	-
Auxiliary Information	Thesaurus	Thesaurus	-
Combination of matching module	Composite	Hybrid	Hybrid
Threshold	User defined	Structural similarity coefficient	User defined
Matching Cardinality	1-1, m-n	1-1, 1-n	1-1, m-n
Reusing preceding match results	Yes	No	No

In the schema matching, some prototypes have been developed such as Cupid [14], COMA [6], Similarity Flooding [16] and Rondo [17]. Cupid is an algorithm of schema mapping between two different representations. It treats the problematic of mapping discovery, which returns mapping elements that identify related element of two schemata. On one hand, Cupid returns results for low scale schemas in an acceptable time [25]. On the other hand, Cupid is inefficient when we compare elements with the number of leaf for the first is double of the second. Similarity Flooding use DOM (Document Object Model) for representing the working schemas. It compares suffix and prefix in common between the graph node labels. The algorithm is efficient with high scale schemas but it returns results after a considerable computing time. COMA can be considered as a framework for schema matching. It allows using many algorithms with different techniques for results rendering. This fully-personalized feature makes it difficult to average user to identify the best combination between different modules. A functional comparison between the preceding representation based algorithms is shown in Table 1. Evaluation of matching algorithm can be also found in [19], [25], and [9]. One more interesting approach uses interactive matching described in [23]. This approach can be very promising since it brings the matching and the mapping to the user interface at the same time. This lack of separation can be as well considered one of the drawbacks of this solution.

Nonetheless, these works are not suitable to the matching of EDI messages. Indeed, EDI messages do not have significant field names, i.e., NAD represents the Address in EDIFACT and 32A represents the amount of the transfer with Swift. Though, the close focus on how an element of an EDI message is defined with: textual description (a short text describing the element's role in the message), data type, constraints (condition depending on the instance value of the element and can influence the value restriction of another element in the message), status (an information indicating if the element's existence in the message is mandatory, optional, …), cardinality (the possible occurrence number of an element within another element in a message). Another important fact concerns the meaning variation of an element due to its location in the message (structural influence). Therefore, we have to identify a new similarity algorithm, which takes into consideration the specific characteristics of EDI message's branching diagram expressed with XML Schema. Furthermore, XML is becoming the promising format for data exchange in B2B and B2C with ebXML [10], semantic web techniques [26], and web Services with SOAP.

3 Our Approach

In this section, we are presenting EX-SMAL (EDI/XML semi-automatic Schema Matching ALgorithm) proposed as a solution for the EDI message's schema matching. The criteria for matching will include data-type, structure, and elements descriptions. Other information related to an element (constraints, status, cardinality) will be taken into account for the future extension of this work.

```
Algorithm EX-SMAL:
Input: S, T: two XML Schemata
Output: set of triplets <S_i, T_j, V_sim>
   With    S_i: an element of S
           T_j: an element of T
V_sim: the similarity value between S_i and T_j
Matching(S, T) {
Convert S and T to tree
For each pair of elements <S_i, T_j>, compute    {
        Basic similarity value.
        Structural similarity value.
        Pair-wise element similarity value.
        }
Filter: eliminate the element pairs having their V_sim
below an acceptation threshold value.
}
```

Fig. 1. Short description of EX-SMAL

The algorithm (Fig.1) can be understood as follows:

- The algorithm takes two XML schemas (S and T) as the input and returns a set of triplets *<es, et, vsim>* in which *es* is an element of S, *et* is an element of T and *vsim* is the pair wise element similarity value between them.
- To match the input schemata, the algorithm convert them into tree (each edge represents the containment relation and each node is an XML schema element, attribute, attributeGroup ...). A tree node is an object characterized by its label, path from root, textual description, data type, constraints, status, and cardinality.
- It computes for each pair of elements *<s, t>*, the Basic similarity value, Structural similarity value, and Pair-wise element similarity value.
- It filters results to eliminate the element pairs having their *vsim* below an acceptation threshold value.

3.1 Basic Similarity

This similarity is computed as the weighted sum of the textual description and data type similarity. We calculate the basic similarity between a pair of elements, each of which comes from the input schema. Because we are dealing with a subset of element criteria, an element has a strong basic similar value with another if their textual description and data type are strongly similar. We can compute the basic similarity of two elements s and t by using the following formula:

$$basicSim(s, t) = descSim(s,t)*coeff\_desc + coeff\_type*dataTypeSim(s,t)$$
where $coeff\_desc + coeff\_type = 1$ and $0 \leq coeff\_desc \leq 1$ and $0 \leq coeff\_type \leq 1$.

3.1.1 Textual Description Similarity

Instead of working on the element label to get the basic similarity of the elements, we choose the textual description associated with each element. Indeed, the element names are not useful for comparing EDI message elements because they are neither significant nor readable. The textual description similarity indicates how much two elements are similar according to their textual description. We use the information retrieval well-known technique such as Vector Space Model [11] to solve this problem.

At first, we start normalizing the textual description by removing stop words, affixes, prefix, and applying stemming techniques. We proceed by extracting the terms' vector containing every term with its associated term frequency in the description. We, then, compute the cosine of the two terms vectors to evaluate a part of the pair wise description similarity. This option is not sufficient to determine the textual description similarity because it takes into account only the term frequency in both descriptions.

Therefore, we add another computing to this description comparison by supposing that each textual description associated with every element of the target schema forms a document. The set of these documents create a corpus which will be indexed. With every single description extracted from a source element, a query is formulated using all the terms after normalization. Then we search the above index to get a set of scores indicating how much the query is relevant to the descriptions in the corpus. The query type we handle takes into account the terms order in the description. The score and the description affinity resulted from the vectors cosine computing will be finally used to calculate the description affinity between two given elements.

3.1.2 Data Type Similarity

We used a static matrix defining the XML schema primitive data type affinity. The values given as the data type affinity between two elements is obtained from the empirical study on those data type format and value boundary. Fig. 2 shows a side of the datatype similarity matrix. These similarity values help to obtain the basic affinity degree of two comparing elements' types.

3.2 Structural Similarity

The structural similarity is computed by using two modules: the structural neighbors computing and the aggregation function **agg**. This computing is based on the fact that two elements are structurally similar if theirs structural neighbors are similar.

Datatype Similarity	String	Normalized String	Duration	DateTime	Time	Date	...	HexBin	Base64bin
String	1.0								
NormalizedString	0.9	1.0							
Duration	0.4	0.4	1.0						
DateTime	0.4	0.4	0.0	1.0					
Time	0.4	0.4	0.0	0.6	1.0				
Date	0.4	0.4	0.0	0.6	0.0	1.0			
GyearMonth	0.4	0.4	0.0	0.4	0.0	0.6			
Gyear	0.4	0.4	0.0	0.2	0.0	0.4			
GmonthDay	0.4	0.4	0.0	0.4	0.0	0.6			
Gday	0.4	0.4	0.0	0.2	0.0	0.4			
Gmonth	0.4	0.4	0.0	0.2	0.0	0.4			
Float	0.6	0.6	0.0	0.0	0.0	0.0			
Double	0.6	0.6	0.0	0.0	0.0	0.0			
Decimal	0.6	0.6	0.0	0.0	0.0	0.0			
Integer	0.6	0.6	0.0	0.0	0.0	0.0			
NonPosInteger	0.6	0.6	0.0	0.0	0.0	0.0			
NonNegInteger	0.6	0.6	0.0	0.0	0.0	0.0			
NegInteger	0.6	0.6	0.0	0.0	0.0	0.0			
PosInteger	0.6	0.6	0.0	0.0	0.0	0.0			
Long	0.6	0.6	0.0	0.0	0.0	0.0			
Int	0.6	0.6	0.0	0.0	0.0	0.0			
Short	0.6	0.6	0.0	0.0	0.0	0.0			
Byte	0.6	0.6	0.0	0.0	0.0	0.0			
UnsignedLong	0.6	0.6	0.0	0.0	0.0	0.0			
UnsignedInt	0.6	0.6	0.0	0.0	0.0	0.0			
UnsignedShort	0.6	0.6	0.0	0.0	0.0	0.0			
UnsignedByte	0.6	0.6	0.0	0.0	0.0	0.0			
Boolean	0.4	0.4	0.0	0.0	0.0	0.0			
HexBin	0.4	0.4	0.0	0.0	0.0	0.0		1.0	
Base64bin	0.4	0.4	0.0	0.0	0.0	0.0		0.0	1.0

Fig. 2. Data type Similarity Matrix

3.2.1 Structural Neighbors

The structural neighbors of an element *e* is a quadruplet *<ancestor(e), sibling(e), immediateChild(e), leaf(e)>* in which: ancestor(e): the set of parent elements from the root until the direct parent of the element e, sibling(e): the set of sibling elements (the elements sharing the same direct parent element) of e, immediateChild(e): the set of direct descendants of the element e, and leaf(e): the set of leaf elements of the sub-tree rooted at e. The choice for these four items defining the structural neighbors of an element is related to many structural observations that we can summarize as follows:

Ancestor elements influence their descendants meaning, however, they do not define the entire structural semantic of a given element. In the Fig. 3, the same label "name" of two elements express different meaning because one is person's name and another is the person's pet's name.

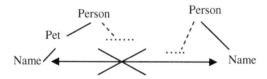

Fig. 3. Ancestral item of an element and structural neighbors

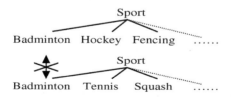

Fig. 4. Sibling item of an element and structural neighborhood

The sibling nodes are interesting to be considered in the structural neighbors. In fact, two elements can perfectly share the same ancestral structure but differ by the influence from their siblings. In the Fig. 4, "Badminton" in the both schemas doesn't share exactly the same meaning despite being similarly grouped in the "Sport" category. One is considered as a general sport like others but another one is quite a kind of "racket sport" due to the influence from "Tennis" and "Squash".

To reinforce the exact semantic of each element, we need to look more detail into the depth of an element. This is related to the fact that the detail of an element resides in its composing elements (**immediate children** and the **last level descendant**). We choose to ponder the immediate children because they define the basic structure of the parent element. The choice of the last level descendant will help us to go through the finest-grained content or intentional detail of an element. In the Fig. 5, the basic information related to a book can be composed of its "feature", "ISBN" and "Author". The detail of the book will be clearer if we focus more into the depth of its three basic elements. We realize that "feature" is the group of "book's title", "book's category" and "book's page number". "Author" can be additionally detailed into "author's name", "author's address", "author's phone number", "author's fax" and "author's e-mail address".

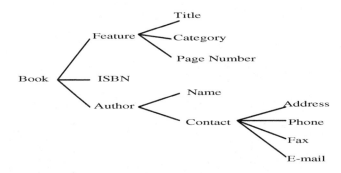

Fig. 5. Direct descendant and leaf items of an element and structural neighborhood

3.2.2 Structural Similarity Value Computing

The structural similarity value of two elements *s* and *t* depends on the similarity value resulting from the comparison of each pair of structural neighbors items (*ancSim(s, t)*, *sibSim(s, t)*, *immCSim(s, t) and leafSim(s, t)*). The similarity value of each structural neighbors pair is computed by using the function *agg(M, thr)* which takes a matrix *M* (containing the set of basicSim(ei, ej) where ei, ej represent the neighbors of s and t respectively) and a threshold value *thr* $\in$ [0, 100] as input. It returns the aggregated value of the input matrix *M*. The function *agg* uses the arithmetic mean (*avg*) and the standard deviation (*sd*) measures of the descriptive probability to compute the variation coefficient (*vc*) of all the values in *M*. Thus, *M* forms a population that contains only the basic similarity values. We use the standard deviation of the arithmetic mean as dispersion measure because it is sharply more exact than others dispersion measures (inter-quartile range, variance, etc). We compute the arithmetic mean *avg* and standard deviation *sd* of *M* respectively with:

$$avg = \frac{\sum\limits_{i=1}^{|ancestor(s)|}\left(\sum\limits_{j=1}^{|ancestor(t)|} M[s_i][t_j]\right)}{|\,ancestor(s)\,|\times|\,ancestor(t)\,|} \quad \text{and} \quad sd = \sqrt{\frac{\sum\limits_{i=1}^{|ancestor(s)|}\left(\sum\limits_{j=1}^{|ancestor(t)|}\left(M[s_i][t_j]-avg\right)^2\right)}{|\,ancestor(s)\,|\times|\,ancestor(t)\,|}}$$

We compute the variation coefficient vc of M by: $vc = \dfrac{sd}{avg}\times 100$. By comparing the calculated variation coefficient with the thr value given by a user, agg decides if the arithmetic mean of M will be the aggregated value of M or not. Wishing that we get the small dispersion of all the values in M around its arithmetic mean, the main target of this agg function is to get a descriptive value from a set of values. With the value thr given by the user we can adjust the aggregated value of the matrix M by eliminating some low values interfering in the arithmetic mean computing. If the user gives $thr \geq vc$, then agg returns avg as the aggregated value of M. If the user gives $thr < vc$, we will eliminate all the values from M below: $avg\left(1-\left(\dfrac{thr}{100}\right)\right)$ interfering in the arithmetic mean computing. We obtain a sub set of values in M and apply again the aggregation function. We apply this computing to all the structural neighbors' items (*ancSim(s,t), sibSim(s, t), immCSim(s, t) and leafSim(s, t)*)[4].

Example: Ancestor item similarity value computing of the element pair s and t.
- *ancestor(s) = {s₁, s₂}*, the parent elements of s
- *ancestor(t) = {t₁, t₂}*, the parent elements of t

M	t_1	t_2
s_1	0.3	0.7
s_2	0.9	0.5

Each of the matrix's case contains a basic similarity value of a pair of elements (e.g. $M[s_1][t_2]=0.7$ is the basic similarity value of s_1 and t_2).

We have *ancSim(s, t) = agg(M, thr)* with *thr* offered by a user. We first compute the arithmetic mean avg of M by the preceding formula: $avg=0.6$. Then, we compute the standard deviation sd of M: $sd=0.223$. Finally, we compute the variation coefficient vc of M by: $vc=37.16$. If the user gives $thr \geq vc$, then agg returns avg as the aggregated value of M. If the user give $thr=10$ which is below the calculated vc, we will eliminate all the values below $avg\left(1-\left(\dfrac{thr}{100}\right)\right)=0.377$, from M. We obtain a sub set of three values in M: {0.7, 0.9, 0.5} and the new aggregated value of M will be the arithmetic mean of that sub set: $avg=\dfrac{0.7+0.9+0.5}{3}=0.7$. In the above case, *ancSim(s, t) = 0.6* when $thr \geq vc$ and *ancSim(s, t) = 0.7* when $thr=10$.

To sum up, depending on the thr value, we'll have the different aggregated value of the same matrix. The rest of the structural neighbor's item similarity (*sibSim(s, t), immCSim(s, t) and leafSim(s, t)*) will be calculated the same way as *ancSim(s, t)* with help from the function *agg*.

3.3 Pair-Wise Element Similarity

After computing the basic similarity value and the structural similarity value for each pair of elements, we can compute their pair wise element similarity value. This value is computed as the weighted sum of the basic similarity value and the structural similarity value. It's proposed as the final similarity value for a pair of elements in our approach. Finally the similarity is calculated with:

similarity(s,t)= basicSim(s, t)*coeff_base   +   structSim(s, t)*coeff_struct
Where $0 \leq coeff\_base \leq 1$, $0 \leq coeff\_struct \leq 1$, And   *coeff_base + coeff_struct = 1*

   As we are using many coefficients in our algorithm, we suggest a method to calculate the best value of each coefficient. We provide the possibility for the user the run the performance batch which helps them to determine the good set of coefficients to use a process of matching. The user can compute the matching between two schemata S and T, depending on the best set of coefficients obtained from the matching between S and S and the one obtained from the matching of T and T. This method gives a help to identify the good set of coefficients to be used in the matching between S and T. Let us assume that $\alpha_0, 0 \leq \alpha_0 \leq 1$, represents the best value for matching a schema S with itself and $Matching(x,y)$ is a bounded function with values in [0,1]. Thus, $\lim_{x \to S} f(Matching(x, S), \alpha) = \alpha_0$ with f is the function of variation for α and $Matching$ (x,S) assuming that all the other coefficients are fix. Let us assume that α_1, $0 \leq \alpha_1 \leq 1$, represents the best value for matching a schema T with itself, $\lim_{x \to T} f(Matching(x,T), \alpha) = \alpha_1$. We aim at finding the best value to match S with T,

$$\lim_{x \to S} f(Matching\ (x,T), \alpha) = \frac{\alpha_0 + \alpha_1}{2}$$, since the function f is continuous then the

closed point to α_0 and α_1 at the same time is the middle point $\frac{\alpha_0 + \alpha_1}{2}$. Thus, we consider this value as the best coefficient to use for matching S and T. we should apply this method to discover all the coefficients used for our matching.

4   Practical Issues

4.1   Implementation Issues

After presenting the sequence of the EX-SMAL Algorithm, we implemented a vertical and horizontal prototype for testing its efficiency with real world examples. The prototype was implemented using Java programming language and using multiple open-sources API such as Lucene (http://jakarta.apache.org/lucene/doc/index.html). First of all, to enable the matching for EDI branching diagram written in XML Schema, we saved the textual information concerning the elements with a correspondent annotation field. According to the algorithm sequence, the six following steps were executed respectively:

Step 1- Tree building: this step consists of converting the algorithm's input, i.e. XML Schemata, into useful tree structures. Each node of these tree is an object containing: the path from the root (e.g. /UNB, /UNB/UNH/DTM,...), the data type, the textual description, and the name of the node (e.g. UNB, UNH, UNZ, ...).

Step 2- Computing basic similarity: this step uses the previously generated data structure and computes the basic similarity using their textual descriptions and their data types. The textual similarity was delegated to the API Lucene (http://jakarta.apache.org/lucene/doc/index.html) and the query type PhraseQuery. This API (version 1.4.0) offers the possibility to generate a term related vector and to calculate the term frequency. Furthermore, we combined the result with the results of PhraseQuery with the cosine of correspondent vectors to find the description similarity. The data type similarities are extracted from a static table showing the affinity degree between different types of XML Schema.

Step 3- Finding of the vectors corresponding to elements' neighbors: this step consists on creating vectors which correspond to the neighbors of each element in the source and target schema. Therefore, 4 vectors are defined respectively for each node in the generated trees covering: *ancestor vector, sibling vector, immediate Child vector, and leaf vector.*).

Step4- Computing structural similarity: in this step, the algorithm calculates the structural similarity between each two nodes of the generated trees. It uses essentially the basic similarity between their neighbors' vectors.

Step-5- Computing final similarity: the results found in Step-2 (basic similarity) and Step-4 (structural similarity) help to calculate the final similarity between each pair of elements in the entries schemata.

Step- 6- Filtering: this last step consists of choosing between the final similarities those being most likely useful. Therefore, every final similarity having a value less than a threshold chosen by the user is going to be eliminated. The set of the remaining similarity can be represented with a line between the used schemata as shown in Fig.6.

The results our similarity matching algorithm can be saved (as XML representation or any other data structure) for a possible future use with the mapping expression [20].

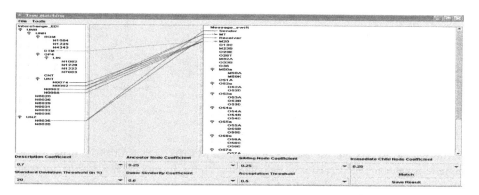

Fig. 6. General view of EDI Translator implementing EX-SMAL algorithm

4.2 Scenario of Test

We tried to apply the EX-SMAL algorithm with some real world examples coming from the EDI's well known standards EDIFACT and SWIFT. The scenario consists on a client using EDI technique in order to pay a supplier invoice. The description of the scenario is defined in Figure 3 and shows the needed EDI schema matching for facilitating the process of message translation. We used the schema of the message MT103 (50 elements/2 levels of depth) from SWIFT and PAYMUL (243 elements/16 levels of depth) from UN/EDIFACT. The choice of matching MT103 with PAYMUL was deliberately made as an extreme example because the two schemata are so much different one from another. We started a test campaign (Batch), using the auto-matching with varying coefficient values, to find the ones which seem to be the best set to use in the future matching process. As we used two schemas (PAYMUL and MT103) with the great structural difference, we recognized that the structural similarity value doesn't help much to refine the pair wise element similarity values. However, to make our structural processing flexible and complete, we observe the structural neighbors of each pair of elements before deciding which value to use (e.g. matching two neighbors without sibling elements will have to make the *coeff_sib* value available for other coefficients values). Thus, we equally dispatch the value of *coeff_sib* over other three coefficients. Finally the value of the remained three coefficients will be the sum of its initial value with a part of value from the *coeff_sib*.

Moreover, we implemented the possibility for the user to run a performance batch which can help to determine the good set of coefficients to use in the matching process. These test campaigns were done by using only the two schemata above and we varied the coefficient values to get the ones which seem to be the best set for us to use in the future matching process. We found a set of values that we fixed as default coefficient values for later matching, *coeff_desc = 0.7, coeff_type = 0.3, coeff_anc = coeff_sib = coeff_immC = coeff_leaf = 0.25, thr = 20, coeff_base = 0.6* and *coeff_struct = 0.4*.

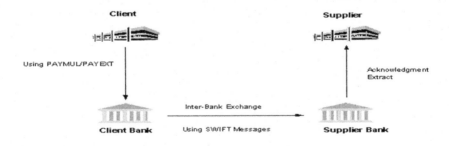

Fig. 7. Scenario of Test

Afterwards, we started the matching between MT103 with PAYMUL using these coefficient values. The precision is calculated with the formula: *Pre= number of true automatic matching / number of total automatic matching*. The accuracy (recall) is calculated with the formula: *Accur=number of true automatic matching/ number of true manual matching*. The matching of MT103 and PAYMUL schema gave us 70% of precision and 25% of recall by using the default coefficients for around 5 minutes of running time (under a PC Pentium IV with 2.8 GHz of speed and 448Mo of RAM.). These results are acceptable in respect with the deliberate examples.

5   Future Work

We envisage enlarging our experiments with a larger number of real-world EDI message schemas. This includes also an empirical study of performance. Furthermore, we should consider improving our prototype to allow user's intervention after the matching process in order to define the mapping expression [22] between the accepted matched elements (i.e. applying the next step after schema matching), generate automatically the needed scripts and code to be applied at run time, store mapping expression using XML syntax to be reused for composition of matching, and couple schema-based matching with instance based matching.

We are seeking, as well, to generalize the EX-SMAL algorithm to fit other domains. Therefore, we are aiming at applying this algorithm with scientific or biological data. Indeed, using description-based schema matching (i.e. Information Retrieval) can be helpful for may other fields outside the E-commerce. Some opportunities can be identified with the ongoing project Kepler (http://www.kepler-project.org) which aims at creating workflow system for scientific data. Therefore, schema matching using our algorithm can help facilitating the processes of connecting actors in the data flow especially when the ports of processes don't have representative names. Another attractive field arises from the need of matching algorithm between schema and trees coming form biological sources. For instance, BioPax (Biological Pathways Exchange) which is an effort to create a data exchange format for biological pathway data have not highly representative element names with very representative description. Thus, applying this algorithm with these exchange schemas can overcome the current issues of mapping between different representations or different formats. Furthermore, the algorithm can be extended to serve as meta-data based schema matching, to be used with database schema and tables where their meta-data offer expressiveness and coherence better than physical names type. Quite often in reality, tables in database models don not carry descriptive names, but are complex encoding of administrative contexts like TAJO2EEN, or VWSG0012Users, which hampers the identification and understanding of the concepts behind them [1].

We started a wide collaboration with teams of Kepler project and SCIA graphical tool [23] in order to reach common goals of schema matching. Further opportunities with biological data and meta-data based matching will be as well studied with collaboration with teams of Biology WorkBench (http://workbench.sdsc.edu/) and CIPRES project (http://www.phylo.org/). This work can include the use of ontology, taxonomy, and dictionaries to improve matching, enable mapping and integration from needed data sources.

6   Conclusion

This algorithm can be classified among the schema based approaches. In fact, it combines between the structural similarity and the textual description similarity. It can differentiate from other approaches with the following particularities. (i) It treats the textual description of the elements, which is richer than other approaches treating the elements labels such as Cupid, COMA, or Similarity Flooding. Effectively, this choice was directed by the particularity of EDI branching diagram. We used some known techniques in Information Search (Information Retrieval) to find the similarity of two elements' descriptions. (ii) It fully treats the structure of an element by covering the structural neighbors' items: ancestors, siblings, immediate Childs, and leafs. However, some limits can be identified for our algorithm such as: (i) Using many coefficients make it hard to be initialized by a non-advanced user and the running time to discover the best coefficients value is difficult and time consuming. (ii) The current algorithm does not take into consideration other important elements of branching diagram such as constraint, status, cardinality, etc. A full solution for an EDI matching algorithm should consider all these elements. (iii) According to the small number of schemata to test, this evaluation should be improved into a large scaled one.

Acknowledgment

We would like to thank Jacques Savoy (Univ. Neuchâtel), Hong Hai Do (Univ. Leipzig), Raj Goswami (Build Fusion), and the member of Lucene Forum for their helpful feedback and suggestions to overcome the technical and implementation difficulties.

References

1. V. Alexiev et al., "Information Integration with Ontologies, Experiences from an Industrial Showcase", Willey & Sons Publisher, West Sussex, England, 2005, ISBN 0-470-01048-7.
2. J. Berlin and A. Motro. "Database Schema Matching Using Machine Learning with feature selection". In Proceedings of the 14th International Conference on Advanced Information Systems Engineering (CAISE'02), May, 2002, Toronto, Ontario, Canada. 15 pages.
3. P. Bouquet, B. Magnini, L. Serafini and S. Zanobini. "A SAT-based algorithm for Neighborhood Matching". Technical Report, DIT-03-005, February, 2003, Informatica e Telecommunicazioni, University of Trento, Italy. 14 pages.
4. U. Chukmol, R. Rifaieh, N. Benharkat, "EX-SMAL: an EDI/XML Schema Matching Algorithm". To appear in the Proceedings of IEEE Conference on E-Commerce.
5. S. Castano, A. Ferrara and S. Montanelli. "H-MATCH: An Algorithm for Dynamically Matching Ontologies in Peer-based Systems". In Proceedings of the SWDB 2003 Conference, September, 2003, Berlin, Germany. pp. 231-250.
6. Hong-Hai Do and E. Rahm. "COMA - A system for flexible combination of Schema Matching approaches". In Proceeding of the 28th VLDB Conference, August, 2002, Hong Kong, China. pp. 610-621.
7. A. Doan, P. Domingos and A. Halevy. "Reconciling Schemas of Disparate Data Sources: A Machine Learning Approach". In Proceedings of ACM SIGMOD International Conference on Management of Data, May 21-24, 2001, Santa Barbara, California, USA. pp. 509-520.
8. A.H. Doan, J. Madhavan, P. Domingos and A. Halevy. "Learning to map between Ontologies On the Semantic Web". In Proceeding of the 11th International Conference on World Wide Web, May 7-11, 2002, Honolulu, Hawaii, USA. pp. 662-673.

9. Hong-Hai Do, S. Melnik and E. Rahm. "Comparison of Schema Matching Evaluations". In Proceedings of the GI Workshop "Web and Database", October, 2002, Erfurt. pp. 221-237.

10. B. Hofreiter, C. Huemer and W. Klas. "ebXML: Status, Research Issues and Obstacles". In the proceedings of the 12th International Workshop on Research Issues in Data Engineering: Engineering e-Commerce/e-Business Systems (RIDE'02), February 24-25, 2002, San José, California, USA. pp. 7 – 16.

11. D.Grossman, O.Frieder, "Information Retrieval Algorithms and Heuristics". Kluwer Academic Publishers, 1998.

12. J. Kang, J. F. Naughton. "On schema matching with Opaque column names and data values". In Proceeding of the 2003 ACM SIGMOD International Conference on Management of Data and Symposium on Principles of Database Systems, 2003, San Diego, California, USA. pp. 205-216.

13. L. Kurgan, W. Swiercz and K. J. Cios. "Semantic mapping of XML tags using inductive machine learning". In Proceedings of the 2002 International Conference on Machine Learning and Application (ICMLA'02), 2002, Las Vegas, Nevada, USA. pp. 99-109.

14. J. Madhavan, P. A. Bernstein and E. Rahm. "Generic Schema Matching with Cupid". In Proceedings of the 27th VLDB Conference, 2001, Rome, Italy. pp. 49-58.

15. J. Madhavan, P. A. Bernstein et al. "Corpus-based Schema Matching". In Proceedings of the 18th International Joint Conference on Artificial Intelligent (IJCAI'03), 2003, Acapulco, Mexico. pp. 49 - 53.

16. S. Melnik, H. Garcia-Molina and E. Rahm. "Similarity Flooding: A Versatile Graph Matching Algorithm and its Application to Schema Matching". In Proceedings of the 18th International Conference on Data Engineering (ICDE), 2002, San Jose, California, USA. 12 pages.

17. S. Melnik, E. Rahm and P. A. Bernstein. "Rondo: A programming Platform for Generic Model Management". In Proceedings of SIGMOD Conference, June 9-12, 2003, San Diego, California, USA. pp. 193-204.

18. R. J. Miller et al. "The Clio project: managing the heterogeneity". SIGMOD Record, 2001, 30(1). pp. 78-83.

19. E. Rahm and P.A. Bernstein. "On Matching Schema Automatically". Technical Report 1/2001, Department of Computer Science, University of Leipzig, Germany, 29 pages.

20. R. Rifaieh and N.A.Benharkat, "Query based Data Warehousing Tool", Proceedings of the 5th ACM international workshop on Data Warehousing and OLAP table of contents, McLean, Virginia, USA, 2002, Pages: 35 – 42.

21. R. Rifaieh and N. A. Benharkat. "An Analysis of EDI Message Translation and Message Integration Problem". In Proceedings of the CSITeA-03, June, 2003, Rio De Janeiro, Brazil, 8 pages.

22. R. Rifaieh and N. A. Benharkat. "A Framework for EDI Message Translation". In Proceedings of the ACS/IEEE Conference AICCSA'03 July, 2003, Tunis, Tunisia, 10 pages.

23. G.Wang, et al., "Critical Points for Interactive Schema Matching", In proc of the 6th Asia-Pacific Web Conference, APWeb 2004, April 14-17, 2004, Hang Zhou, China.

24. L. Xu, D. W. Embley. "Discovering Direct and Indirect Matches for Schema Elements". In Proceedings of the DASFAA 2003 Conference, March, 2003, Kyoto, Japan. pp. 39-46.

25. M. Yatskevitch. "Preliminary Evaluation of Schema Matching Systems". Technical Report, DIT-03-028, November, 2003, Department of Information and Communication Technology, University of Trento, Italy. 13 pages.

26. L. Zamboulis. "XML Schema Matching & XML Data Migration & Integration: A Step towards the semantic web vision". Technical Report, October, 2003, School of Computer Science and Information Systems, Birkbeck University of London, England. 20 pages.

A Lightweight Model-Driven Orchestration Engine for e-Services

Johann Oberleitner, Florian Rosenberg, and Schahram Dustdar

Distributed Systems Group, Institute of Information Systems,
Vienna University of Technology
{joe, rosenberg, dustdar}@infosys.tuwien.ac.at

Abstract. Service-oriented Computing (SoC) in general, and e-service orchestrations in particular have the potential to increase reuse and to ease maintainability. Typically, interoperating e-services require orchestration efforts, which should be accomplished outside the application logic itself. In this paper we present a novel MDA-based approach for generating orchestrations of e-services, enabling the automatic generation of e-service orchestrations based on UML models. Secondly, such orchestrations may include GUIs. Thirdly, we discuss our execution environment supporting heterogeneous e-service orchestrations, including Web services, COM, CORBA, and .NET objects. Such heterogeneous software system landscapes are very common today, where many (legacy) applications still exist and are not wrapped as e-services, nor BPEL process descriptions are available.

Keywords: Model-Driven Approach, Service Orchestration, e-Services.

1 Introduction

Today, there is a growing recognition that the Service-oriented Computing (SoC) paradigm [1], including its property of loose-coupling, facilitates higher flexibility of interoperable information systems. To increase reuse and to ease maintainability, interoperating e-services require orchestration efforts, which should be accomplished outside the application logic itself.

In this vein, recent Model-driven Development [2] efforts, provide a viable conceptual framework allowing software or e-service generation, with (ideally) minimal extra coding efforts. Current ambitions in research and industry are, therefore, aimed at moving e-service development towards a higher level of abstraction, where models of e-services and their orchestrations are modeled and the code is generated thereafter. On the one hand, Service-oriented Architectures (SOA) gain wider acceptance as a paradigm for loose coupling of software services distributed on the Internet. On the other hand, activities carried out by humans increasingly require higher flexibility and new ways of supporting loosely-coupled work teams and its involved team members. Today, both users of e-services, i.e., humans or other e-services, are not integrated well enough to leverage the full potential of SoC.

C. Bussler and M.-C. Shan (Eds.): TES 2005, LNCS 3811, pp. 48–57, 2006.
© Springer-Verlag Berlin Heidelberg 2006

The contribution of this paper is threefold. We provide: a) an MDA-based approach for generating orchestrations of e-services, enabling the automatic generation of e-service orchestrations based on UML models; b) the integration of GUIs in such orchestrations; and c) an execution environment supporting heterogeneous e-service orchestrations, including Web services, COM, CORBA (by using [3]), and .NET objects. Such heterogeneous software system landscapes are very common today, where many (legacy) applications still exist and are not wrapped as e-services, nor BPEL process descriptions are available. Nevertheless, such heterogeneous systems require integration into larger orchestrated systems.

The remainder of this paper is structured as follows. Section 2 provides a motivating example from an application domain where we evaluated the viability of our implementation. Section 3 outlines the modeling support provided in our implementation. Section 4 discusses the execution engine which processes UML state- and activity-diagrams and generates required orchestrations. Section 5 presents related work. Section 6 concludes the paper and outlines our future work.

2   Motivating Example

We motivate our model-driven orchestration approach by considering the following example from the hospital domain. When a patient arrives at the hospital several departments and different specialists are involved in the diagnosis. Each department has different, heterogeneous software systems — ranging from applications using COM or CORBA components, and systems offering Web services — which have to be used to make a diagnosis. Some parts of the workflow are performed manually, by entering data using a GUI, other steps are performed automatically, e.g., storing blood-specific data or x-ray results in the database. In addition, it might be necessary to include data from previous examinations that are not stored in-house. Therefore, external services need to be queried. Our scenario, a routine meniscus surgery, has the following workflow: (1) When the patient arrives at the hospital, her personal data is collected and entered in the hospital information system by using a GUI application. On finishing the registration, the health insurance data (containing information from previous diagnoses, etc.) is collected from the insurance company by using their Web services, and stored in the patient record. (2) After the registration process, a doctor is briefing the patient where previous diagnoses and illnesses are discussed and upcoming examinations are clarified. The doctor directly enters important notes to the hospital information system by using the provided GUI application. (3) The standard procedure for a meniscus surgery is to take blood and make x-rays of the necessary parts. The order of these examinations is not important. Due to the high amount of data, the x-rays result is not stored in the hospital information system directly, it is archived in a special database in the radiology department and linked with the patient record. (4) Then, the patient has to go back to the doctor to do the final medical examinations and to discuss the

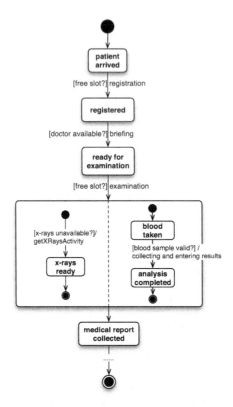

Fig. 1. Hospital Workflow State Diagram

results of the blood sample and the x-rays. The notes from the doctor are again directly entered into the system.

A simplified version of this workflow is shown in Figure 1 as a UML state-chart diagram. We use this model throughout the paper to explain the concepts of our model-driven orchestration approach.

3   Model Driven Approach

In the next sections we describe our orchestration models and how these models are transformed to our internal representation so that our execution engine can process it.

3.1   Modeling Support

We support UML state machines as well as activity diagrams to build a model based orchestration for services. Both diagram types are important for building complex business processes. While state machines are suitable when explicit states can be identified and activities infer transitions between these states, activity diagrams are preferred when no states can be identified or each activity would require the introduction of pseudo-states. Furthermore, in state diagrams, the state of an orchestration is always explicit. This explicit state offers support for long-running transactions, which require such explicit points to wait for other activities (e.g., user input).

For state-charts, we support most constructs provided by the UML 1.5 standard [4]. In particular, simple states, composite states to structure an orchestration, history states, concurrent states, initial (start) and final (end) states and transitions, eventually restricted by guards, are supported. In the example depicted in Figure 1, we have used an initial state, multiple simple states, one concurrent state with two nested child states and multiple transitions. To execute application logic associated with states or transitions, references to an action may be linked to state entry, state exit or the firing of transitions. An action itself may be modeled by an activity diagram or another state machine, or we refer to an invocation. Most UML modeling tools support these links directly in the model.

According to Figure 1, when a new patient arrives, the first state is entered. When a free registration slot is available, the registration process is initiated, in which the nurse enters the patient data by using a GUI application which will be invoked by the `registration` action. Such actions can be modeled by activity diagrams which may include service invocations, but also processing steps of a GUI. Actions included in a model can refer to GUIs to fill and retrieve data and to steer the control flow. For instance, user decisions (e.g., pressing buttons) in a GUI may directly be reflected in the control flow of the orchestration.

After several state transitions, the patient is waiting for a free examination slot, which leads to states running concurrently: the right part models the blood examination, whereas the left one models how to deal with required x-rays images which is handled by the `getXRaysActivity` in case the x-rays have not already been available in the system. After both results are available, the concurrent states are left and the medical report is prepared.

Actions invoked on state entry, state exit and on state transitions, are either service invocations, activity diagrams or new state machines. The highest flexibility among these possibilities is provided by executing activity diagrams, as can be seen in Figure 2. Actions in this diagram are activated when no recent x-ray images are available. It models the possibilities of providing a recent x-ray image, (1) either by scanning the one brought by the patient, or (2) by requesting it via Web service from a medical specialist or (3) create one in-house by doing an x-ray.

Unlike standard design processes, we require that the models are complete, since the various models are the single source of input. Due to space restrictions, our illustrations are just simplifications of real models. There must not be any informal actions or guards. For our model in Figure 1, this means that the guard [doctor available] must refer to system variables, for instance, [exists (doctorAvailable)]. This expression evaluates to true if there exists a global system variable doctorAvailable.

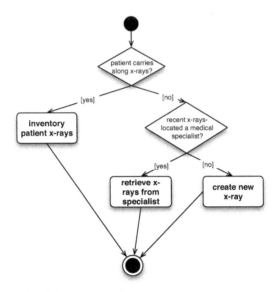

Fig. 2. X-Rays Activity Diagram

Modeled orchestrations can be exposed as composite services, therefore, two special actions for receiving input messages and replying output messages have to be included in the diagrams. These actions are parameterized by name and type of the message parts and variable names which are used to refer to within the orchestration.

3.2   Transformation Tool

The models can be created with any UML standard compliant modeling tool, which supports XMI [2] export. Our execution engine, however, does not process XMI directly but requires a data source which supports sequential data, such as relational databases or XML files.

We have built a transformation tool, which converts XMI files to our sequential representation. States and transitions of state machines are parsed and stored in tabular form. Table 1 shows a subset of the generated state entries. Nesting of states is handled with the state type column for which concurrent or composite states can possess child states. The example shows the examination state from Figure 1 which contains several child states processed concurrently. The child states themselves are composites.

Table 2 depicts how transitions are stored by the transformation tool. For instance, the transition that leads to the **x-rays ready** state in Figure 1 has a guard and invokes the `getXRaysActivity` action.

Activity diagrams are also stored in one action table that stores the name of the action and invocation parameters. To support control flow actions, the transformation tool assigns unique incremental numerical ids to each action in

Table 1. Transformed State Example

state name	state type	parent state	initial child state	entry action	exit action
examinations	concurrent	-	-	-	-
x-ray examination	composite	examinations	initial x-rays	-	-
initial x-rays	initial	x-ray examination	-	-	-
x-rays ready	simple	x-ray examination	-	-	-
x-rays available	final	x-ray examination	-	-	-

Table 2. Transformed Transition Example

transition name	source state	target state	transition action	guards	trigger events
getXRays	x-rays init	x-rays ready	getXRays-Activity	exists (s::xrays)	-
anonymous	x-rays ready	x-rays available	-	-	-

the activity diagram. The execution engine uses these ids to dynamically select the next action.

4 Execution Engine

We have built our lightweight execution engine for the .NET platform to execute the models described in the previous sections. In this section we describe the mechanisms to process models stored in a format provided by the transformation tool. The aforementioned tables act as input to the execution engine.

4.1 Processing State Machines

Processing a state machine is initiated by creating an instance of the **State-Machine** class. This instance fetches the state and transition tables into memory. After the instantiation of the state machine, initial states are immediately entered and followed to the innermost nested state. Figure 3 shows parts of the class diagram for processing state machines.

Transitions between states are triggered by events. We support different kinds of events, primarily GUI events caused by user interactions or custom events caused by programmatic actions. In case one of these events happens, a transition is fired and the target state becomes activated.

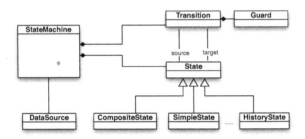

Fig. 3. Execution Engine Class Diagram

On each state entry or state exit, as well as on transitions, an action can be executed. These actions may refer to activity diagrams, state machines, or service invocations. There is no particular difference, if a simple state is entered or if a nested state in a composite state is entered. Furthermore, we emit additional .NET events on state entry, state exit or state transition. This allows the execution of recurring actions for each transition arc without polluting the process models by referring to the same activity diagrams over and over. For instance, if a user is not allowed to enter another state dependent on the context of the data, event handlers may cancel the transition.

In addition to an action that may be executed when a transition event has fired, a guard expression can be provided. This guard expression returns a boolean value and is evaluated before a state exit or an optional transition activity is started. In case the guard evaluates to false the whole transition is canceled and the old state is restored.

Furthermore, our engine also supports history states. A history state stores in which substate a composite state resided before the composite state is left. When the history state is entered again the previous state is restored. Concurrent states split the execution in multiple paths, which can be executed in parallel. The child states of a state of type `concurrent` are in turn composite states that require an explicit initial and an explicit final state. When a concurrent state is entered, the initial states of each child state are entered. A concurrent state is left when each concurrently processed child state has reached a final state. One drawback of our implementation, however, is that we do not support transitions from one concurrent state to another.

4.2   Processing Activity Diagrams

Fine-grained actions may be modeled with UML activity diagrams. Our execution engine processes sequences of actions stored in the data source of the `actiongroup` tables. Figure 4 shows the classes involved in processing of action groups. To execute these action-groups an instance of type `ActionGroup` is created. Similar to states and transitions of state machines, the sequence of actions is loaded on initialization of the action-group. Actions themselves are realized with the flyweight pattern [5]. For each single action within a sequence of actions

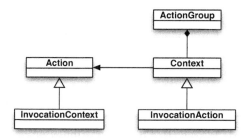

Fig. 4. ActionGroup Class Diagram

a `Context` object is created that parses and stores the parameters originating from the action description in the data source. The classes that implement the actions themselves inherit from the `Action` class.

When an action-group shall be executed a loop processes each context object that in turn delegates the execution to the action object. The context provides not only access to the parameters of the action but supports also access to variables with different scopes, either system global, statemachine-local, or local to an activity diagram. Furthermore, the control flow within an activity diagram may be modified by modifying some predefined fields of the context. We have predefined various action classes that have different tasks:

Control-flow actions: Some actions deal with modifying the flow within the sequence of actions. The execution engine supports an if-then-else construct, too. One parameter provides the conditional expression that is evaluated at runtime. These expressions refer to any variables stored in the context and test its existence, support relational operators for comparison of numbers and strings, and may use logical operators to build complex expressions. Another action *ReturnToOldState*, allows that a transition may be canceled by setting a context flag.

StateMachine actions: A small number of actions allow starting sub-state-machines that will either block the current machine or can also run in parallel.

Container actions: Some actions allow reading and writing to arbitrary variables provided by a blackboard. Actions and the state machines can then access these variables.

Domain-specific actions: We have used the execution engine to also integrate GUI elements. Hence, we have built a couple of actions that load and show GUI forms and other actions that allow modification of GUI widgets.

Invocation actions: Services can be executed by using one of the invocation actions (for CORBA, .NET, COM or Web services). The targets of these calls are configured externally. The execution of further actions may be blocked by another action that supports waiting for notifications.

New action types can easily be added by providing an action class which implements execution semantics and a context class that parses and stores the configuration parameters.

5   Related Work

To the best of our knowledge, there are currently no existing model-driven orchestration approaches, which focus on the integration of heterogeneous services that also include GUI applications.

In the workflow and BPM (Business Process Management) area, numerous approaches exist that focus on coordinating work through software. Most of these approaches are not capable of invoking different components such as Web services, COM, DCOM, Java, EJB. The few existing approaches, such as JOpera [6] or JBPM [7] use proprietary languages and tools for modeling, whereas we rely on using standardized tools (UML) to model our workflows. Furthermore, these tools only support Web services and Java technologies.

Newer approaches, inspired by the service-oriented architecture (SOA), focus on the orchestration and composition of Web services into higher-level processes and composed services. Currently, BPEL [8] is increasingly used for the orchestration of Web services [9]. We believe that one of the major disadvantages of BPEL is that the activity types in the orchestration are limited to Web services only and that there is currently no modeling standard for BPEL processes. BPEL-J [10], a joint effort of BEA and IBM, tries to combine BPEL with Java by adding activities, called *Java Snippets*, which allow to embed Java code into the process and allow to interact with J2EE components. Our decision not to use BPEL as execution language has several origins: Firstly, BPEL is not designed for combining service invocations and human-centric interactions. Secondly, existing BPEL execution engines are rather heavyweight, while our execution engine has only small requirements on the environment and may potentially be executed on PDAs.

Executable UML [11] is one research direction in the MDA area focusing on building directly executable models of software systems which are used as input to execution engines. Usually these approaches focus on rather small domain-specific areas, such as embedded systems [12]. Our approach, however, focus on the integration of heterogeneous services.

6   Conclusion and Future Work

Orchestrating e-services provided by different systems is increasingly important for heterogeneous systems. Current implementations do not focus on a model-driven orchestration of services provided by heterogeneous systems and the integration of GUI based applications. Based on an example from the medical domain, we presented our model-driven approach for specifying service orchestrations, which allow the invocation of various services implemented in .NET, CORBA and COM. Furthermore, a service can even be a GUI application integrated into the orchestration. A previous version of the system is already in use in one hospital in Austria.

We plan to improve modeling the support. Currently, exception handling is only supported by nesting diagrams, which is tedious to do with modeling tools.

By specifying rollback points and compensation actions, nesting can be avoided in the model, and is automatically supported by the transformation tool.

The future work in this area includes porting the execution engine from .NET to Java, which offers the flexibility, to additionally integrate and invoke components and applications written in Java and EJB. Furthermore, a Java solution allows us to invoke functionality implemented with common component models in the invocation classes through the Vienna Component Framework (VCF) [13].

References

1. Papazoglou, M.P.: Service-oriented computing: concepts, characteristics and directions. In: Proceedings of the Fourth International Conference on Web Information Systems Engineering. (2003) 3–12
2. Frankel, D.S.: Model Driven Architecture – Applying MDA to Enterprise Computing. OMG Press (2003)
3. Oberleitner, J., Gschwind, T.: Transparent Integration of CORBA and the .NET Framework. In: Proceedings of On the Move to Meaningful Internet Systems 2003: CoopIS, DOA, and ODBASE (DOA). (2003)
4. Object Management Group (OMG): Unified Modeling Language (UML), Version 1.5. http://www.omg.org/technology/documents/formal/uml.htm (2004)
5. Gamma, E., Helm, R., Johnson, R., Vlissides, J.: Design Patterns: Elements of Reusable Object-Oriented Software. Addison-Wesley (1995)
6. Pautasso, C., Alonso, G.: From web service composition to megaprogramming. In: 5th International Workshop on Technologies for E-Services (TES). (2004) 39–53
7. JBoss: Java business process management. http://jbpm.org/ (2005)
8. BPEL: Business Process Execution Language for Web Services Version 1.1. http://www.ibm.com/developerworks/library/ws-bpel/ (2003)
9. Pasley, J.: How BPEL and SOA are changing web services development. IEEE Internet Computing **9** (2005) 60–67
10. BEA Systems Inc. and IBM Corp.: BPELJ: BPEL for Java. ftp://www6.software.ibm.com/software/developer/library/ws-bpelj.pdf (2004)
11. Mellor, S.J., Balcer, M.J.: Executable UML – A Foundation for Model-Driven Architecture. Addison-Wesly (2002)
12. Raistrick, C., Francis, P., Carter, J.W.C., Wilkie, I.: Model Driven Architecture with Executable UML. Cambridge University Press (2004)
13. Oberleitner, J., Gschwind, T., Jazayeri, M.: The Vienna Component Framework: Enabling composition across component models. In: Proceedings of the 25th International Conference on Software Engineering (ICSE). (2003)

Ad-UDDI: An Active and Distributed Service Registry

Zongxia Du[1], Jinpeng Huai[1], and Yunhao Liu[2]

[1] School of Computer Science,
Beihang University, Beijing, P.R. China
duzx@act.buaa.edu.cn
[2] Dept. of Computer Science,
Hong Kong Univ. of Science and Technology, Hong Kong
liu@cs.ust.hk

Abstract. In SOA (Service Oriented Architecture), web service providers use service registries to publish services and requestors use registries to find them. The major current service registry specifications, UDDI (Universal Description, Discovery and Integration), has the following drawbacks. First, it replicates all public service publications in all UBR (Universal Business Registry) nodes, which is not scalable and efficient, and second, it collects service information in a passive manner, which means it waits for service publication, updating or discovery request passively and thus cannot guarantee the real-time validity of the services information. In this paper, we propose an active and distributed UDDI architecture called Ad-UDDI, which extends and organizes the private or semi-private UDDIs based on industry classifications. Further, Ad-UDDI adopts an active monitoring mechanism, so that service information can be updated automatically and the service requestors may find the latest service information conveniently. We evaluate Ad-UDDI by comprehensive simulations and experimental results show that it outperforms existing approaches significantly.

1 Introduction

Web services based on service-oriented architecture (SOA) provide a suitable technical foundation for interoperability and integration of applications [1, 2]. To make the web services accessible to users, service providers describe their interfaces with WSDL [3] and publish the description to service registries, so that service requestors may find them conveniently [4]. As a result, service registries play an important role in SOA. Most today's service registries comply with UDDI [5] (Universal Description, Discovery and Integration) specifications, whose initial focus was geared to working as UBR (Universal Business Registry), a master directory for all public web services. However, as shown in Fig. 1, Su Myeon Kim et. al. showed their observations on public web services [6] on the monitoring result about UBR, in which only 34% of the Web Services (WS) are valid. Here a 'valid' Web Service means a WS with a URL where a WSDL file is retrievable. Furthermore, a large portion of the downloaded WSDL files are invalid due to syntax errors. On the other side, very few organizations update their service information after their first publication. According to the report in [3, 6], there are approximately 16% valid Web Services down weekly. As a result, the availability of service information in UBR is not good.

C. Bussler and M.-C. Shan (Eds.): TES 2005, LNCS 3811, pp. 58–71, 2006.
© Springer-Verlag Berlin Heidelberg 2006

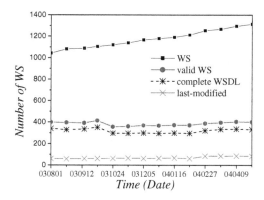

Fig. 1. Web Services in UBR[*]

We have following observation on current UDDI service registry in SOA. First, it replicates all web service publications in all UBR nodes, which is not suitable for the large number of services. Second, it collects service information in a passive manner, which means it waits for service publication, updating or discovery request passively. Consequently, the real-time validity of the service information is not guaranteed.

In this paper, we propose an active and distributed UDDI architecture called Ad-UDDI, which extends and organizes the private or semi-private UDDIs based on industry classifications. Further, Ad-UDDI adopts an active monitoring mechanism, so that service information can be updated automatically and the service requestors may find the latest service information conveniently. We evaluate Ad-UDDI by comprehensive simulations and experimental results show that it outperforms existing approaches significantly.

The rest of this paper is organized as follows. Section 2 presents an overview of related works. Section 3 introduces the design of Ad-UDDI. We show our experimental results in Section 4 and conclude the work in Section 5.

2   Related Work

Flexible resource management is a key point for the collaboration between partners. Traditional centralized resource management framework have limitations both in their failure tolerance and scalability [7]. Recent years, there are more and more attention changed to the distributed framework [8, 9] for scalability and flexibility.

UDDI v3.0.2 released in 2004 recognizes the needs for multiple registries, as well as the interactions among registries [5]. Due to the large number of registries focusing on various interests, service publication and discovery becomes challenging. In addition, UDDI v3 provides subscription mechanisms to enable affiliate registry to obtain changed information of a root registry, but there is no approach to get the real status of the services except waiting passively for the updating requests from service providers.

In ADS (Advertisement and Discovery of Service Protocol) issued by IBM [10], service descriptions are collected by UDDI crawler rather than being manually

---

[*] The copyright of the data and related analysis belongs to the authors of [6] and we have obtained the permission from Su Meyeon Kim for using the data in this paper.

published. The design of crawler borrows the idea from the web search engine and sets the file, *svcsadvt.xml*, to the root of Web Server. When a crawler finds such a file, it collects the corresponding service information of the web site. However, when the web crawler goes ahead according to the hyperlink in the web page, there is no hyperlink information in the web service description. Therefore, the diffusing of crawler is much difficult. UDDIe [11] is an extended registry for web services, which exploits the lease time of each service to ensure the availability of service information in registries. However, the lease time and availability of service is dependent on the relationship established in advance between UDDIe and the service providers, and there is no method for checking the real availability of services.

MSWSDI [12] is a part of the ongoing METEOR-S [13] project. It is a scalable P2P registry infrastructure for semantic publication and discovery of web services. It employs an ontology-based approach to organize the registries and enable domain-based semantic classifications for all web services. Each of these registries supports semantic discovery of the web services. In MSWSDI, the relationship among the registries is managed based on a Registries Ontology. Because the Registries Ontology needs specific management and maintenance, the organization of the registries is not trivial. Authors in [14] proposed a federated architecture for P2P web-services, in which a federation for UDDI-enabled peer registries is employed in a decentralized fashion. Service providers publish their services on a centralized UDDI and then join service syndication. Obviously, a single point of failure cannot be avoided. Also, no mechanism is designed for getting real status of services.

3 Design of Ad-UDDI

In this section, we introduce the active monitoring mechanism of Ad-UDDI and its distributed architecture. With the active monitoring mechanism, Ad-UDDI improves the availability of service information. With the distributed architecture, Ad-UDDI reduces the performance bottlenecks and improves the availability of service registries.

3.1 Design of Active Monitoring

The availability of service information in registries is of great importance. However, due to the fact that few organizations update their published information in registries on time [6], a certain mechanism has to be applied to monitor the service status and update the information in registries automatically.

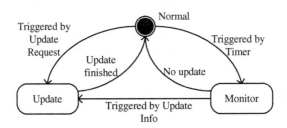

Fig. 2. The state chart of Ad-UDDI

In this design, a registry server, called Ad-UDDI server, checks the real time status of services and collects the service information periodically. The state chart of the Ad-UDDI server, as shown in Fig. 2, consists of three states, *Normal*, *Update* and *Monitor*. In the *Normal* state, the Ad-UDDI server waits for periodically monitoring triggers or incoming requests. In the *Monitor* state, the Ad-UDDI server initiates a monitoring request to the service provider. In *Update* state, the Ad-UDDI server updates the service information in Ad-UDDI based on the returned messages from providers.

Once triggered by a timer, the Ad-UDDI transfers from the *Normal* to the *Monitor* state and starts checking the real status of services. If the monitored service has not been updated yet, the Ad-UDDI returns to the *Normal* state triggered by a 'nonUpdate' message. If the monitored service is updated, the Ad-UDDI transfers from the *Monitor* state to the *Update* state, executes the information updating process. After that, the Ad-UDDI returns to the *Normal* state again. Another way, the Ad-UDDI in a *Normal* state transfers into the *Update* state if it is requested by the providers.

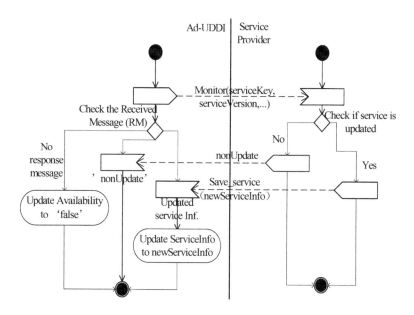

Fig. 3. The interaction process of active monitoring

Figure 3 illustrates the interaction process of the active monitoring mechanism. The Ad-UDDI server sends a 'Monitor' message to a service provider periodically, containing the registered service name, service key and service version. The service provider checks each item in the 'Monitor' message with its own. To simplify the handling process and reduce the load, only service name, key and version are compared. If they are identical, a message of 'nonUpdate' is returned. Otherwise, new service information is sent to the Ad-UDDI server via a 'save_Service' message which is an API interface of UDDI. On receiving a 'nonUpdate' message, the Ad-UDDI server terminates the present monitor thread. On receiving a 'save_Service' message, the Ad-UDDI server conducts the service updating process. If there is no message returned within given time period, the service is considered to be unavailable and the Ad-UDDI server will step into 'Update', claiming the unavailability of the service.

It is noteworthy that an unavailable service might be caused by a network failure, a temporal invalidation of the provider's server, or the undeployed service. Therefore, we should deal with the unavailable service based on the service monitoring strategies, instead of a simple deletion. In our implementation, monitoring strategy is often as follows: 1) service information is to be cancelled after 10 times of monitoring without any returned message; 2) on receiving a returned message, the Ad-UDDI updates the service information accordingly and resets the service as available; 3) on receiving a service discovery request, the Ad-UDDI server searches in available services only.

3.2 Design of Distributed Architecture

The Ad-UDDI adopts a three-layered structure of distributed service registry, as Fig. 4. The top layer is the root registry layer, in charge of managing the Ad-UDDI service information. The root is a special Ad-UDDI server, in which every Ad-UDDI server in the middle layer publishes its own information as a web service. In addition, we do not let this layer publish and monitor business services so as to reduce its work load. The middle layer is the business service registry layer, in which all Ad-UDDI servers are initiated following GICS (Global Industry Classification Standard) [15]. Normally, the business services belonging to a classification are registered in corresponding Ad-UDDIs and multiple industry classification services may be registered in one Ad-UDDI. The bottom is the service layer, in which every service publishes their information to one or more Ad-UDDI based on to their service type and industry classification.

The solids in Fig. 4 show the publishing relationship, such as business services publish their information to the corresponding Ad-UDDI and Ad-UDDIs publish their information to the root. The dash lines in the middle layer denote the neighboring relationship, such as Ad-UDDI 1, 2 and 4 have established the neighboring relationship according to their classification ("Transportation"). The dash lines in the bottom layer show the interaction relationship between services.

There are mainly five operations in such distributed architecture, including *adding* and *closing* of an Ad-UDDI, *Ad-UDDI neighbor maintenance*, *service querying*, and *service updating*.

a) Adding a new Ad-UDDI

In case of adding a new Ad-UDDI, it sends its basic information to the root registry, and search in the root registry for other Ad-UDDIs in the same industry classification. The new Ad-UDDI then requests to establish neighboring relationship with existing same category Ad-UDDIs. When a request is granted, the two Ad-UDDIs record the other side's information. Finally, once the neighboring relationship is set up, the publishing and discovering of services are performed within the middle layer without accessing to the root registry. Therefore, while the root is a single point of failure, there is little influence on the publishing and discovery of web services. In that case, only adding or closing an Ad-UDDI will be fail. The protocol of adding a new Ad-UDDI is presented in Fig. 5.

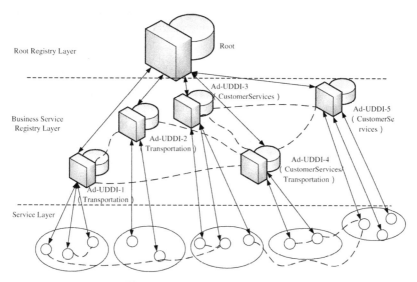

Fig. 4. The distributed architecture

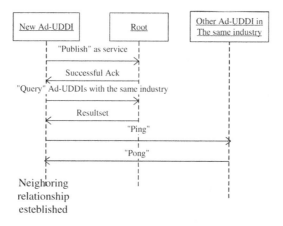

Fig. 5. The interaction protocol of adding an Ad-UDDI

b) Closing an Ad-UDDI

In case of closing an Ad-UDDI, the following four modes are possible in this design: 1) to close an Ad-UDDI directly, discarding all service stored without contacting the root registry; 2) discard all service information but inform the root registry of its unavailability; 3) transfer all service information to its neighbors before closing without informing the root; 4) move all service information to neighbors, sends a closing request to the root registry, and waits for permission. Obviously, the complexities of above four modes increase in order. In our design, an Ad-UDDI might be closed by anyone of them. Although the fourth one is usually encouraged, the first mode is used when an Ad-UDDI fails to connect with the root registry center due to the network failure. Figure 6 illustrates the fourth mode interaction protocol.

c) Neighbor Maintenance

Neighboring relationship among the Ad-UDDIs is established when a new member joins. When an existing member leaves, it is possible that it does inform its neighbors. In this design, we require the root registry center monitors the status of all Ad-UDDIs and broadcasts the updated information to all Ad-UDDIs in the same category using the subscription method in UDDI v3.

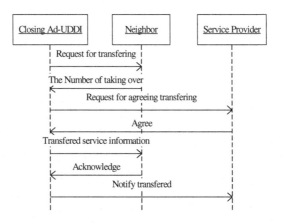

Fig. 6. The interaction protocol of closing an Ad-UDDI

d) Service Querying

Each Ad-UDDI maintains the service information published in it and deals with the service query from service requestors. To improve the service querying efficiency, each Ad-UDDI caches the recent searching results. On receiving a service query, an Ad-UDDI looks up its cache repository. If the desired service is found, the Ad-UDDI returns the result to the requestor and terminates the query. If there is no target found, the Ad-UDDI goes on querying in local and neighboring repositories, and then stores the querying results into local cache after returning the results to the requestor.

e) Diffused Updating of Service Information

In this distributed structure, the updating of the service information is extended to all neighboring Ad-UDDIs whose local caches have cached related service information. This procedure is called the diffused updating of the service information.

With both the diffusing updating and the active monitoring mechanism, the state-chart of the Ad-UDDI in Fig. 2 is extended into the one shown in Fig. 7. Having updated the service information locally, the Ad-UDDI broadcasts an updating message to its neighbors, so that the neighboring Ad-UDDIs can update corresponding information in their caches.

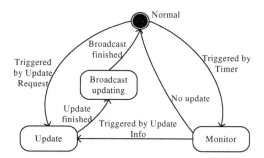

Fig. 7. The extended state chart of Ad-UDDI

3.3 Implementation Experiences

The implementation of Ad-UDDI prototype server contains four repositories, i.e. the Local Service Information Repository (LSIR), the Local User Information Repository (LUIR), the Neighbor Ad-UDDI Information Repository (NAIR) and the Cached Service Information Repository (CSIR), as illustrated in Fig. 8. The LSIR and the LUIR are similar with those in UDDI servers. The NAIR and the CSIR are implemented purposely for the Ad-UDDI. The NAIR holds the information of neighboring Ad-UDDIs. The NAIR stores the neighbor's name, its access point, its industry classification, etc. The CSIR caches the service information which has been queried by requestors before. The major functional blocks to manage the information in the repositories are as follows.

User Manager manages the information of the service providers and requestors registered in current Ad-UDDI. It accepts registration requests from new users, updates the information for registered users, and implements access control.

Scheduler invokes various managers according to requests (such as publishing / querying).

Local Service Information Manager publishes the service information to the local service repository, queries the service information in local repository and updates information in local repository.

Active Monitor connects the service providers who published their services in this Ad-UDDI, monitors the real-time service status, and updates the service information.

Cached Service Information Manager manages and maintains the CSIR, and caches the returned queries. On receiving a query requests, it searches in the CSIR for the matched service. It also guarantees the synchronization of the information. At last, it manages the cache size. When too much information is cached, the least recently requested ones will be deleted.

Diffusing Updater performs the information synchronization among the Ad-UDDIs. When the information of LSIR is changed, it propagates the information to the neighbors according to the information in the NAIR to update the cached service information of other Ad-UDDI servers. When updating requests come, it forwards the request to the Cached Service Information Manager for updating.

Diffusing Querier propagates the service querying requests to neighbors to get more candidate services.

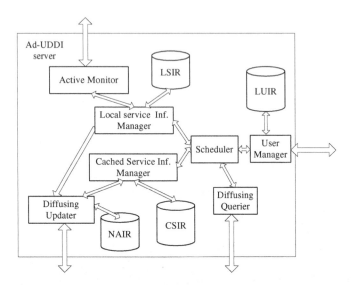

Fig. 8. The architecture of Ad-UDDI server

In addition, an Ad-UDDI provides four interfaces including local service monitoring interface, service synchronizing interface, diffusing query interface and user request interface.

Among them, local service monitoring interface is used to send the active monitoring request to the service provider periodically and wait for the reply messages. The service synchronizing interface is used to send the updated service information to its neighbor Ad-UDDIs when its local service information is changed. If the neighbors have cached this service information, they need update the cached information. The service diffusing query interface is used to diffuse the local query request to its neighbors, so that querying can be processed in a larger scope. The user request interface is similar with the interface of traditional UDDI, which is used to receive and process the diversified requests from users.

4   Performance Evaluation

To evaluate the performance of the Ad-UDDI approach, we coded a simulator using Java, in which a certain number of Ad-UDDIs, service providers and requestors are connected to form a mesh network to simulate the situation of Internet.

We use BRITE [16] to generate topologies up to 2,000 nodes with random connection. The network delay between every two nodes is calculated according to the shortest path along the physical network topology. Each service is remarked by its name, key, version, type, access point, etc. In each run, a number of services with diversified types are deployed into the network.

Each Ad-UDDI in the simulation is able to register the service information in several industries, while every industry classification can be registered into several Ad-UDDIs. We distribute the Ad-UDDIs into finite industries and publish the services into

Ad-UDDIs based on their types. The root registry is a special Ad-UDDI node, which only registers the information of the Ad-UDDI services without receiving the publication of the business services. On the other hand, we simulate UDDI as a centralized registry without active monitoring method and all services publish their information to it. In this section, we introduce our performance metrics, and then the simulation results.

4.1 Performance Metrics

The basic function of the Ad-UDDI is to find available web services matching requestors' demands. To better evaluate the Ad-UDDI design, we use the following metrics: *available rate, success rate, average response time,* and *total traffic cost.*

The *Available Rate* is defined as the ratio of the requests which successfully find desired and available services at the first return out of all requests. In real B2B environment, the service requestor tends to use the service information directly from the service registry, so the invalidity of discovered service information is very likely to cause the crash of B2B applications. Therefore, the available rate is an important metrics in B2B applications.

The *Success Rate* is defined as the ratio of the requests which successfully find desired and available services out of all requests.

The *Average Response Time* is defined as the average time elapsed from the issuance of a query till a desired and available service is found. If no appropriate service is found, the query ends after searching all candidate services which have the same service type with the request.

The *Total Traffic Cost* is defined as the traffic of messages incurred by queries and responses. If the active monitoring mechanism is adopted, the traffic of monitoring and diffusing updating messages is also considered. We will record the total traffic cost in 30 days with 10,000 requests.

4.2 Results

In the first simulation, we apply the active monitoring mechanism, where 1,000 services are distributed into randomly selected nodes. We set 10 Ad-UDDIs as the registries with 5 industry classifications and generate 10,000 requests every 3 days to trace the evolution of the available rate of the queries. The results in Fig. 9 show that the available rate of information in the registry without active monitoring mechanism drops to a very low level after 30 days. With the help of AD-UDDI, the available rate stays in a relatively high level, which means the requestors can always find available needed services at the first return.

The second simulation is implemented to analyze the response time distribution of the requests. The service number and the Ad-UDDIs number are the same as in the first simulation. We disperse 10,000 requests in 30 days and record their response time. Figure 10 plots the success rate against the response time. With an *interval* of active monitoring is 1 day, 96% requests get available services within 1.9 seconds. Without Ad-UDDI design, only 69% requests can get the available ones within such time period, and more than 15% requests never find available ones. Larger monitoring interval leads to longer response time, but smaller query overhead. Figure 11 plots the response time against system size. The results show Ad-UDDI design is scalable when the number of nodes increases.

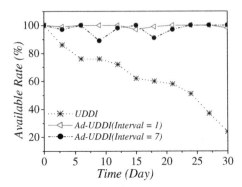

Fig. 9. Available rate v.s. time with 1000 services

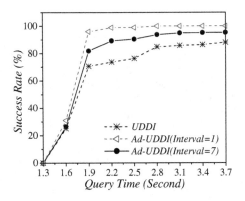

Fig. 10. Success rate v.s. Query Time

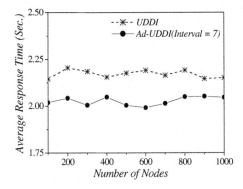

Fig. 11. Response time v.s. number of services

We then explore the total traffic cost with different service numbers by recording the cost in 30 days with 10,000 requests. According to Fig. 12, the total traffic cost is slightly increased with larger number of services. With the same number of services, the query traffic with Ad-UDD is much smaller than without active monitoring. In Fig. 13, we show the relationship between the total traffic cost and the monitoring interval with 100 and 1,000 services involved respectively. If we set the monitoring interval as 1 day, there will be a lot of monitoring cost. On the other side, without monitoring, we save the monitoring messages but more services have to be checked in order to find an available service, which means the traffic cost of queries will increase. There is an obvious trade-off between monitoring and query traffic.

Combined with Fig. 9, shorter interval between two monitoring process leads to higher available rate, but brings larger monitoring traffic cost, as shown in Fig. 13. We can conclude that the weekly monitoring is a good balance between available rate and the traffic cost. Furthermore, we can set different interval for various services. The service with more importance needs smaller interval.

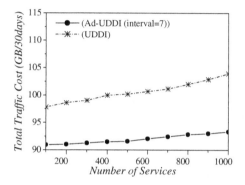

Fig. 12. Total traffic cost v.s. number of services

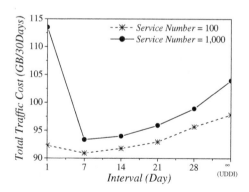

Fig. 13. Total traffic cost v.s. interval

5 Conclusion

Aiming at resolving the low validity of the public UDDI, we propose an active and distributed registry, Ad-UDDI, to provide available service information. In this design, the service information is distributed among multiple registries and thus the single point of failure and bottleneck in one public UDDI is reduced. In our approach, the root registry takes charge of managing the Ad-UDDI services without any business services, so the burden of root registry is lightened. The distributed architecture of Ad-UDDI may serve as a basic method of connecting the private or semi-private UDDIs. With the active monitoring mechanism, the real-time availability of the service information in the Ad-UDDI is significantly improved.

Acknowledgement

This work was supported in part by China NSFC 90412011, by Hong Kong RGC Grants DAG 04/05 EG01, and by Microsoft Research Asia.

References

1. M. Luo, M. Endrei, P. Comte, P. Krogdahl, J. Ang, and T. Newling, Patterns: Service_ Oriented Architecture and Web Services. http://www.redbooks.ibm.com/abstracts/ sg246303.html?Open. 2004.
2. D. Booth, H. Haas, and F. McCabe. Web Services Architecture. http://www.w3.org/ TR/ws-arch/. 2004.
3. E. Christensen, F. Curbera, G. Meredith, and S. Weerawarana. Web Services Description Language(WSDL) 1.1. http://www.w3.org/TR/wsdl. 2001.
4. Z. Du, J. Huai, Y. Liu, C. Hu, and L. Lei. IPR: Automated Interaction Process Reconciliation. in Proceedings of the International Conference on Web Intelligence(WI2005). 2005.
5. L. Clement, A. Hately, C.v. Riegen, and T. Rogers. Universal Description Discovery & Integration (UDDI) 3.0.2. http://uddi.org/pubs/uddi_v3.htm. 2004.
6. S.M. Kim and M. C. Rosu. A survey of public web services. in Proceedings of the 13th International Conference on the World Wide Web (WWW'04). 2004.
7. M. Cai and M. Frank. RDFPeers: A Scalable Distributed RDF Repository based on A Structured Peer-to-Peer Network. in Proceedings of the 13th International Conference on World Wide Web (WWW'04). 2004.
8. W. Hong, M. Lim, E. Kim, J. Lee, and H. Park. GAIS: Grid Advanced Information Service based on P2P Mechanism. in Proceedings of IEEE International Symposium on High Performance Distributed Computing 2004 (HPDC 2004). 2004.
9. L. Xiao, X. Zhang, and Z. Xu. On Reliable and Scalable Peer-to-Peer Web Document Sharing. in Proceedings of the 16th International Parallel and Distributed Processing Symposium (IPDPS 2002). 2002.
10. W. Nagy, F. Curbera, and S. Weerawaranna. The Advertisement and Discovery of Services (ADS) protocol for Web services. http://www-128.ibm.com/developerworks/library/ ws-ads.html?dwzone=ws. 2000.
11. A. ShaikhAli, O.F. Rana, R.J. Al-Ali, and D.W. Walker. UDDIe: An Extended Registry for Web Service. in Symposium on Applications and the Internet Workshops SAINT2003). 2003.
12. K. Verma, K. Sivashanmugam, A. Sheth, A. Patil, S. Oundhakar, and J. Miller, METEOR–S WSDI: A Scalable P2P Infrastructure of Registries for Semantic Publication and Discovery of Web Services. Journal of Information Technology and management, 2005.

13. A.A. Patil, S.A. Oundhakar, A.P. Sheth, and K. Verma. Meteor-s: web service annotation framework. in Proceedings of the 13th International Conference on World Wide Web (WWW 2004). 2004.

14. M.P. Papazoglou, B.J. Kramer, and J. Yang. Leveraging Web-Services and Peer-to-Peer Networks. in Proceedings of the 15th International Conference of Advanced Information Systems Engineering, (CAiSE2003). 2003.

15. GICS Structure and Sub-Industry Definitions. http://www.msci.com/equity. 2005.

16. A. Medina, A. Lakhina, I. Matta, and J.W. Byers. BRITE: An Approach to Universal Topology Generation. in Proceedings of the 9th International Workshop on Modeling, Analysis, and Simulation of Computer and Telecommunication Systems(MASCOTS2001). 2001.

WS-Policy for Service Monitoring

Luciano Baresi, Sam Guinea, and Pierluigi Plebani

Dipartimento di Elettronica ed Informazione,
Politecnico di Milano, Piazza L. da Vinci, 32 - 20133 Milano, Italy
{baresi, guinea, plebani}@elet.polimi.it

Abstract. The paper presents a monitoring framework for WS-BPEL processes. It proposes WS-CoL (Web Service Constraint Language) as a domain-independent language, compliant with the WS-Policy framework, for specifying user requirements (constraints) on the execution of Web service compositions. WS-Policy and WS-CoL provide a uniform framework to accommodate both functional and non-functional constraints, even though the paper only addresses non-functional requirements. It concentrates on security, which is one of the most challenging QoS dimensions for this class of applications.

1 Introduction

Originally, *service-centric* computing relied on the simple and essential service-oriented paradigm, where service providers, service users, and service directories were the only players. Recently, many proposals have tried to extend the service-oriented approach with issues related to composition, conversation, monitoring, and management [1]. In particular, this paper focuses on extending the basic features with the capability of monitoring the execution of composed Web services (i.e., WS-BPEL processes), as a way to assess both their functional correctness and quality of service. Monitoring should address both functional and non-functional aspects and might involve different parties: clients may be interested in probing the services they use, providers may assess the services they offer, but also third party entities might be involved to offer neutral monitoring capabilities and collect historical data.

The paper introduces a monitoring approach capable of probing both functional and non-functional requirements. Functional requirements predicate on the correctness of the information exchanged between the WS-BPEL orchestrator and the selected services; non-functional requirements are about aspects directly related to how well the service works in terms of, for example, security, transactionality, performance, and reliable messaging. In order to probe such a wide range of requirements, the execution must be analyzed: (1) before invoking the service, that is, before the message to invoke it exists, (2) after producing the message, but before reaching the target service, (3) before the return message reaches its destination, and (4) after reaching it. The first two cases cover the flow from the WS-BPEL orchestrator to the target service, while the other two cases deal with the opposite flow.

The approach presented in this paper concentrates on client-side monitoring and relies on WS-Policy [2], the emerging standard to define Web service requirements, to express the *monitoring policies* associated with WS-BPEL processes, that is, the user

C. Bussler and M.-C. Shan (Eds.): TES 2005, LNCS 3811, pp. 72–83, 2006.

requirements (constraints) on running Web services compositions. All constraints are written in WS-CoL (Web Service Constraint Language), a domain-independent language for monitoring assertions.

The paper also describes a prototype component, called *Monitoring Manager*, that can be used to extend existing platforms for service offering and invocation[1] with monitoring capabilities.

Even though the approach is general, the paper only addresses non-functional aspects, and specifically it concentrates on security, one of the most challenging QoS dimensions for deploying Web services systems. The approach is exemplified on a simple case taken from the common scenario of online book shopping. BookShop is an online bookshop that uses a WS-BPEL process to coordinate all the steps that must be taken to interact with its clients. Here, we concentrate on the service invocation the process makes to OnlineBank to register credit-card transactions. We require that this invocation be encoded using the 3DES algorithm and be pursued only if the total amount to be charged is less than the amount defined in the user's preferences. In fact, BookShop maintains a repository of user preferences to simplify the process of buying books and registers the client's credit-card and a money cap. A money cap is useful when a client wants to avoid spending more than a certain amount of money in a single transaction.

The paper is organized as follows. Section 2 briefly discusses the WS-Policy framework and how related specifications can be used along the Web service life-cycle. Section 3 introduces the monitoring approach adopted to check the proposed policies for monitoring. Section 4 introduces WS-CoL, our assertion language adopted to express non functional requirements. Section 5 presents the architecture of the monitoring framework and exemplifies how it works. Section 6 briefly surveys related approaches and Section 7 concludes the paper.

2   WS-Policy and Policy Lifecycle

WS-Policy [2] is emerging as the standard way to describe the properties that characterize a Web service. By means of this specification, the functional description of a service can be tied to a set of assertions that describe how the Web service should work in terms of aspects like security, transactionality, and reliable messaging. According to [3], an assertion is defined as "an individual preference, requirement, capability or other property", and the WS-Policy document is in charge of composing such assertions to identify how a Web service should work. These assertions can be used to express both functional aspects (e.g., constraints on exchanged data), and non-functional aspects (e.g., security, transactionality, and message reliability). So far, a couple of languages, namely WS-SecurityPolicy and WS-ReliableMessaging Policy, have been proposed as a set of WS-Policy-compliant domain dependent assertions. Similarly, as discussed in Section 4, we propose WS-CoL (Web Service Constraint Language), as a domain-independent language to express monitoring constraints.

As stated in [4], policies can be defined by several actors and during different phases of the Web service life-cycle (Figure 1). Besides implementing the application, service developers also specify the properties that must hold during the execution regardless

---

[1] For example, existing service buses.

of the platform on which the services will be deployed (*service policies*). On the other hand, service providers specify the features supported by the application servers on which services are deployed. (*server policies*). The intersection of service and server policies results in *supported policies*, which define the properties of the services deployed on a specific platform. Finally, Web service users state the features that should be supported by the services they want to invoke (*requested policies*). By combining requested policies and supported policies, we obtain the so called *effective policies*. Approaches to policy intersection are discussed in [4, 5, 6].

In this paper, we do not concentrate on policy intersection, but on the result produced by policy intersection, that is, the effective policies. Effective policies represent the set of assertions that specify the properties of a Web service deployed on a particular server and invoked by a specific user. The Web service to which effective policies apply is linked by definition and it can be a simple Web service or a WS-BPEL process. Once effective policies are derived, services should be monitored at runtime to guarantee that they offer the service levels stated by their associated policies. So, in this paper we propose a framework capable of monitoring effective policies expressed using WS-Policy.

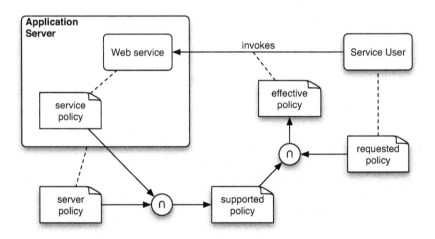

Fig. 1. Ws-Policy definitions and attachments

WS-PolicyAttachment [7], one of the elements of the WS-Policy framework, supports the policy life-cycle described above by defining how a WS-Policy document can be tied to an XML document that represents the subject for which the policy holds. Notice that the assertions included in the effective policy can be applied at different levels of granularity: process level, branch of execution level, service invocation level, message level, or internal variable level. Hereafter, for simplicity, we suppose that all the effective policy assertions work at the same level and, more precisely, at the service invocation level. If the considered service is a WS-BPEL process, policies can be attached to some of the service invocation activities.

3   Monitoring Approach

Runtime monitors [8] are the "standard" solution to assess the quality of running applications where suitable probes control the functional correctness and the satisfaction of QoS parameters. Our monitoring approach borrows its grounding from assertion languages, like Anna (Annotated Ada [9]) and JML (Java Modeling Language [10]), and is also based on the idea that we want to reuse as much existing technology as possible as a means to increase its diffusion and acceptability[2].

The tradeoff between monitoring and performance might be influenced by many different factors. We cannot define a strict relationship between WS-BPEL processes and monitoring directives. Users must be free to change them to cope with new and different needs. For example, the execution of these processes in different contexts might require a heavier burden in terms of monitoring, while when selected services are well-known and reliable, users might decide to privilege performance and adopt a looser monitoring framework.

These considerations led us to propose monitoring directives as stand-alone (external) *monitoring policies* rendered in WS-Policy (see Section 2). These constraints do not belong to the workflow description, that is, the WS-BPEL process, but they are weaved with it at deployment-time. Besides the gain in flexibility, with different sets of monitoring policies that can be associated with the same process, this solution also allows us to keep a good separation between business and control logics.

The weaving process is governed by BPEL^2, which instruments the original WS-BPEL specification to make it apply the monitoring policies. The pre-processor parses all the monitoring policies selected for the particular process. For each policy, the embedded location indicates the point of the process in which BPEL^2 substitutes the WS-BPEL invoke activity with a call to the monitor manager, which is then in charge of evaluating the policy and call the service if it is the case. BPEL^2 also adds an initial call to the monitoring manager, to send the initial configuration (such as the priority at which the process is being run) to initialize it, and a final call to communicate it has finished executing the business logic and that resources can be released.

BPEL^2 produces a fully-compliant WS-BPEL specification, which is deployed instead of the original one. Monitoring policies are not actually intertwined with the original process. BPEL^2 only adds calls to the monitoring manager. This means that policies can change without re-instrumenting the process.

After the weaving process at deployment-time, monitoring policies can be switched on and off at runtime [11]. Special-purpose parameters, like *priority*, allow the designer to select those policies that are to be checked at run-time (they must be a subset of those selected at deployment time). Notice that the priority associated with monitoring policies must not be confused with the `preference` defined in the WS-Policy framework. The preference defines the internal order among policies, while the priority is used to define if a policy must be monitored. For example, if a policy has priority lower than the current one (i.e., the one set by the monitoring manager), the manager skips its execution and calls the actual service directly. The monitoring manager, the component

---

[2] The current implementation of the approach as "external" component can be seen as a feasibility study before embedding this technology in a standard WS-BPEL engine.

that oversees the application of the monitoring policies, has a dedicated user interface that lets the designer change its current priority and thus dynamically modify the impact that monitoring has on the execution.

4   Web Service Constraint Language

The *Web Service Constraint Language*, hereafter WS-CoL, is a domain-independent policy assertion language for specifying user requirements (constraints) on the execution of Web services. Ws-CoL is a standard assertion language augmented with special-purpose features to retrieve "external" data. It distinguishes between *data collection* and *data analysis* to differenciate the phase in which information is collected (from external sources, if needed) from the phase in which stated expressions are evaluated against collected values. Data can be collected from the process directly (e.g., internal variable), but they can also come from external sources (e.g., exchanged SOAP messages, metering tools).

Internal variables are accessed by means of the following instruction:

$$\$<\texttt{name\_of\_variable}>\backslash<\texttt{part\_of\_variable}>$$

As in the WS-BPEL specification, a variable is an instance of an XML schema. Since a variable can be composed of several parts, this instruction allows us to access the different parts.

If data come from external sources, called data collectors, we use the following instruction:

```
\return[Int|String|Boolean](WSDL, OpName, <parameters>)
```

It defines how to retrieve the information that originates outside the process. We suppose that data collectors are Web services, therefore the instruction's parameters have the following meanings:

- WSDL represents the URL of the WSDL related to the requested data collector. For example, in Figure 2, WSDL_XPATH indicates a data collector capable of extracting data from XML snippets according to an XPath expression.
- OpName represents the operation supported by the data collector. In the example of Figure 2, applyXPATH is an operation that returns the value corresponding to an XPath expression.
- <parameters> represents the set of values requested by the operation. In the example of Figure 2, the applyXPATH operation requires two arguments: an XPath expression and the file in which the information is stored (we suppose that up.xml contains the user preferences).

So far, we support data collectors returning an integer, string, or boolean. These intructions can be nested to filter (or compose) the data gathered from different sources.

Data analysis can be carried out by different data analyzers. The WS-CoL concrete syntax can be translated into different abstract representations that correspond to different analysis engines. In this paper, we concentrate on a specific engine implemented using xlinkit [12] and CLiX [13]. WS-CoL complies with the WS-Policy framework, and assertions based on Ws-CoL can be included in a WS-Policy file.

1. Policy attachment:

```
<wsp:PolicyAttachment xmlns:wsp="...">
    <wsp:AppliesTo xmlns:wsal="...">
      <wscol:MonitoredItems xmlns:wscol="...">
        <wscol:MonitoredItem type="precondition"
            path='XPATH expression to WS-BPEL invoked activity'/>
      </wscol:MonitoredItems>
    </wsp:AppliesTo>
    <wsp:PolicyReference
        URI="http://www.bookshop.it/policies#BookShopPolicy/>
</wsp:PolicyAttachment>
```

2. Policy definition:

```
<wsp:Policy xml:base="http://www.bookshop.it/policies"
              wsu:Id="BookShopPolicy"
        xmlns:wsp="..."
        xmlns:wsu="...">
    <wsp:All xmlns:wsse="..."
              xmlns:wscol="...">
      <wsse:Confidentiality>
        <wsse:Algorithm type="wsse:AlgSignature"
            URI="http://www.w3.org/2000/09/xmlenc#3des-cbc"/>
      </wsse:Confidentiality>
      <wscol:Expression>
          ($ChargeRequest\amount) <=
          \returnInt(WSDL_XPATH, applyXPATH,
                    '\\userpref\moneyCap', up.xml)
      </wscol:Expression>
    </wsp:All>
</wsp:Policy>
```

Fig. 2. Ws-Policy example

Figure 2 shows a possible effective policy attachment[3], where policy BookShopPolicy is applied to all the subjects identified by the XPath expression in the MonitoredItem tag. The type attribute specifies when the expressions included in the policy must hold. More in details, the effective policy, which must be satisfied when the credit card is about to be charged, is defined in the second part of the Figure: the BookShopPolicy states both functional and non-functional properties. In the example, we use an assertion that complies with Ws-SecurityPolicy to specify that all exchanged messages be encrypted using "3DES" as the encryption algorithm. Moreover, functional requirements impose that every time clients are ready to pay for their books, the order cannot exceed the money cap. This last constraint is rendered in the WS-CoL assertion included in the Expression tag: the amount of money of the current purchase (ChargeRequest) must be less than or equal to the moneyCap of the current user's preferences (uP).

---

[3] Namespaces are not included for the sake of readability.

Notice that the expression $ChangeRequest\amount retrieves the cost of the purceise from the corresponding WS-BPEL internal variable, while \returnInt (WSDL_XPATH, applyXPATH, '\\userpref\moneyCap', up.xml) retrieves the maximum amount the user is willing to spend, from the preferences file named up.xml.

5   Monitoring Manager

The proposed monitoring component, called *Monitoring Manager*, is simple and extensible in terms of the data analyzers it can use for verifying functional and non-functional properties at run-time. Simplicity has been chosen over other guidelines, such as performance, due to its prototypical nature. The *Monitoring Manager* is composed of four principal components (see Figure 3): the *Rules Manager*, the *Configuration Manager*, the *External Monitors Manager* and the *Invoker*.

The UML collaboration diagram of Figure 4 shows how such components interact during the execution of a WS-BPEL process if the monitoring of pre-conditions is required. When BPEL[2] produces the instrumented version of the process, it adds an initial call to the manager (1) that sets up the monitoring activities by creating a specific configuration in the Configuration Manager (2). This configuration contains all the policies that are selected for the process.

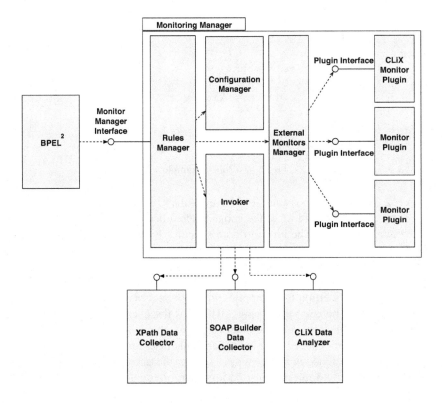

Fig. 3. Interaction with the Monitoring Manager

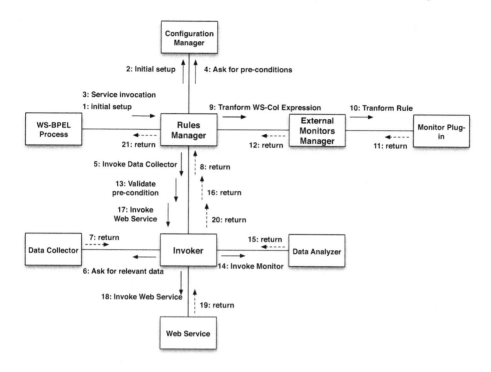

Fig. 4. Interactions among the main elements of the monitoring manager

After setup, the execution of the actual business logic commences. If the instrumented process needs to invoke a service that must be monitored, it invokes the Monitoring Manager in its place (3). The manager is sent the data that are to be analyzed and the information required to invoke the Web service that the manager is wrapping. The Rules Manager extracts the expressions associated with the service invocation from the Configuration Manager. In Figure 2, an encryption policy and a functional pre-condition are associated with the OnlineBank service invocation. This means that when the monitoring of these properties is requested by the instrumented process, their appropriate expressions are extracted from the Configuration Manager (4).

The pre-condition is a functional property that must be verified prior to constructing the SOAP message that must be sent to the OnlineBank service. The encryption policy is a non-functional property that must be verified after the SOAP message has been constructed and prior to sending it to the OnlineBank service. If we consider return messages, the approach works similarly.

When a policy has to be checked, the Rules Manager starts by confronting the policy's property with the global process execution priority. This is done to decide whether the policy should be monitored or if the requested monitoring activity can be ignored. In our example, we can imagine the process execution priority is "4" while the monitoring rule's priority is "5". This means that the required monitoring activity cannot be ignored.

If a policy is to be monitored, the Rules Manager analyzes the expressions to see if additional data must be obtained prior to effective analysis (5,8). If additional data is needed (meaning a \returnString, \returnInt, etc. is present in the WS-CoL expression), the Invoker is called to interact with the specified external data collectors (6,7). Once all the data has been obtained, the Rules Manager asks the appropriate external monitor plugin to translate the WS-CoL expression and the data into the formats the external monitor (in this case the CLiX monitor) is capable of interpreting (9,10,11,12). Once this translation is completed, the appropriate data analyzer is invoked (13,14,15,16) and the Rules Manager waits for a response. If the response is that the property is valid, (this is the case in Figure 4) the Rules Manager proceeds by asking the Invoker component to call the Web Service that would have been called originally (17,18,19,20,21). If the data analyzer responds by saying that the property is not valid, a standard exception is raised to the instrumented process which can then decide for some recovery strategies[4].

At this point the manager proceeds to the monitoring of the SOAP message that is to be sent to the OnlineBank service, to see if it is encrypted as stated in the encryption policy (see the policy example in Figure 2), in other words using "3DES". Notice that even for this policy the monitoring approach is the same as described before. In fact, when the instrumented version of the WS-BPEL process is created, the encryption policy is translated into WS-CoL, to make it interpretable by the manager. This means that, potentially, a generic WS-Policy assertion can be translated into a WS-CoL assertion in order to express how the assertion can be monitored.

In particular, the policy is translated into two different WS-CoL expressions, one for the outgoing message and one for the returning message. Both are sent to the manager during the initial setup phase and stored in the Configuration Manager. If we consider the WS-SecurityPolicy assertion included in our example:

```
<wsse:Confidentiality>
   <wsse:Algorithm type="wsse:AlgSignature"
      URI="http://www.w3.org/2000/09/xmlenc#3des-cbc"/>
</wsse:Confidentiality>
```

The corresponding WS-CoL expression for the outgoing message is:

```
<wscol:Expression>
   \returnString(WSDL_XPATH, applyXPATH,
      '\\Envelope\body\EncryptedData\EncryptionMethod\@Algorithm',
      \returnString(WSDL_SOAP_DC, getSOAP,
                    'BookShopPolicy', 'Data')
      ) == 'http://www.w3.org/2000/09/xmlenc#3des-cbc';
</wscol:Expression>
```

In this expression, we suppose to have an XPath data collector (WSDL_XPATH) and a SOAP data collector (WSDL_SOAP_DC). The first retrieves data corresponding to XPath expressions. The second generates the SOAP message that correspond to invocations of external Web Services.

The WS-CoL expression uses two nested \returnStrings. The inner one, by using the SOAP data collector, asks to produce an encrypted SOAP message using the encryption policy stated in the initial WS-Policy file and the data received from the

---

[4] Recovery strategies are not part of this paper and are our future work.

instrumented process. Amongst these data is the WSDL of the service that must be invoked with the encrypted message. This is needed for understanding the structure of the SOAP message that has to be built. The outer \returnString, extracts a value (whose location is specified using an XPath expression) contained in the header of the just newly built SOAP message. In the meanwhile, the encrypted SOAP message, as built by the SOAP data collector, is kept untouched in the Invoker, preventing it from being modified. This is fundamental since it represents the actual message that will be sent to OnlineBank, once its correct encryption is proven. The value extracted by the XPath data collector is eventually confronted with "3DES" by the CLiX data analyzer. If the message results to be encrypted correctly, the Invoker is instructed to forward the message to the OnlineBank service. If the message is not encrypted correctly, the system raises an exception that is passed to the instrumented process.

The return message received by OnlineBank must also be monitored for correct encryption. Once the return message is received by the Invoker, it is copied and passed to the XPath data collector that extracts the header element to confront it with "3DES". Once again, we use a WS-CoL expression containing a \returnString call to the XPath data collector. The extracted values are then passed to the CLiX data analyzer. If the message results to be correctly encrypted, it is passed to the SOAP data collector for decryption, after which the result of the decryption is forwarded to the instrumented process. If the message is not correctly encrypted, an exception is raised and passed to the instrumented process.

Generally speaking, given a generic WS-Policy assertion to be monitored, if a data source capable of identifying the effects of such an assertion exists, we can derive a Ws-CoL expression. This expression instructs the monitoring manager to state if the non-functional properties the user requires are satisfied.

6   Related Work

The research initiatives undertaken in the field of web service monitoring share the common goal of discovering erroneous situations during the execution of services. They differ, although, in a number of ways: degree of invasiveness, abstraction level at which they work, reactiveness or pro-activeness, and nature of erroneous situations they are capable of discovering.

For example, Spanoudakis and Mahbub [14] have developed a framework for monitoring requirements of WS-BPEL-based service compositions. Their approach uses event-calculus for specifying the requirements that must be monitored. Requirements can be behavioral properties of the coordination process or assumptions about the atomic or joint behavior of deployed services. The first can be extracted automatically from the WS-BPEL specification of the process, while the latter must be specified by the user. Events are then observed at run-time. They are stored in a database and the run- time checking is done by an algorithm based on integrity constraint checking in temporal-deductive databases.

Lazovik et al. [15] proposes another approach based on operational assertions and actor assertions. The first can be used to express properties that must be true in one state before passing to the next, to express an invariant property that must hold throughout all the execution states, and to express properties on the evolution of process variables. The second can be used to express a client request regarding the entire business process, all the providers playing a certain role in the process execution, or a specific provider. The system then plans a process, executes it, and monitors these assertions. This approach shares with ours the fact of being assertion-based. Once the assertions are inserted, it is completely automatic in its setup and monitoring. It lacks although the possibility of dynamically modifying the degree of monitoring. It also lacks adoptability since it is based on proprietary solutions.

A third approach, Cremona (Creation and monitoring of WS-Agreements) project [16] is the only one which, so far, is based on WS-Policy, embedded in WS-Agreement declarations, to express the non-functional requirements. WS-Agreement [17] is a standardization effort of the Global Grid Forum that defines an agreement protocol based on XML. This standard defines agreements for interfaces, security and quality of service properties. Cremona provides a framework that simplifies the definition, the management and the run-time monitoring of the state of the agreements.

7   Conclusions and Future Work

Even if WSDL represents the standard way to define what a Web service does, many efforts are now focusing on languages that can complete such a description by considering aspects that are not directly related to how a service should be invoked. WS-Policy, and all the other languages included in the WS-Policy framework, represent one of the most well-known attempts and, due to its flexibility, could be a candidate to become the future standard. For these reasons, in this work, we decided to extend the WS-Policy framework by proposing WS-CoL, as a domain-independent assertion language.

This paper is only a first proposal to embed monitoring directives into policies. The first implementation of the Monitoring Manager and the experiments with the (complete) example presented in this paper gave promising results, but the approach needs further analysis and a wider set of case studies to fully assess its soundness. Rules driving the automatic translations from WS-Policy assertions to Ws-CoL expressions are under development. All these activities are facilitated by the availability of our monitoring framework.

References

1. M. P. Papazoglou and G. Georgakopoulos. Service-oriented computing: Introduction. *Communication ACM*, 46(10):24–28, 2003.
2. J. Schlimmer (ed.). Web Services Policy Framework (WS-Policy Framework). www.ibm. com/developerworks/library/specification/ws-polfram/, September 2004.
3. A. Nadalin (ed.). Web Services Policy Assertions Language (WS-PolicyAssertions). www. ibm.com/developerworks/library/ws-polas/, May 2003.
4. N. Mukhi, P. Plebani, T. Mikalsen, and I. Silva-Lepe. Supporting Policy-driven behaviors in Web services: Experiences and Issues. In *Proceedings of the Second International Conference on Service Oriented Computing (ICSOC2004)*, New York, NY, USA, 2004.

5. P. Nolan. Understand WS-Policy processing. Explore Intersection, Merge, and Normalization in WS-Policy `http://www.ibm.com/developerworks/webservices/library/ws-policy.html`.
6. K. Verma, R. Akkiraju and R. Goodwin. Semantic Matching of Web Service Policy. `http://lsdis.cs.uga.edu/ kunal/publications/Semantic Policy-SWDP-final.pdf`.
7. C. Sharp (ed.). Web Services Policy Attachment (WS-PolicyAttachment). `www-128.ibm.com/developerworks/library/specification/ws-polatt/`, September 2004.
8. N. Delgado, A. Q. Gates and S. Roach. A Taxonomy and Catalog of Runtime Software-Fault Monitoring Tools . *IEEE Transactions on software Engineering*, pages 859-872, December, 2004.
9. D. C. Luckham. Programming with Specifications: An Introduction to Anna, A Language for Specifying Ada Programs. *Texts and Monographs in Computer Science*, Oct 1990.
10. G. T. Leavens, A. L. Baker, and C. Ruby. Preliminary Design of JML: A Behavioral Interface Specification Language for Java. *Department of Computer Science, Iowa State University, TR 98-06-rev27*, April, 2005.
11. L. Baresi, C. Ghezzi and S. Guinea. Smart Monitors for Composed Services. *In Proceedings of the 2nd International Conference on Service Oriented Computing*, 2004.
12. XlinkIt: A Consistency Checking and Smart Link Generation Service. *ACM Transactions on Software Engineering and Methodology*, pages 151–185, May 2002.
13. CLiX: Constraint Language in XML. `www.clixml.org/clix/1.0/`.
14. K. Mahbub and G. Spanoudakis. A Framework for Requirements Monitoring of Service Based Systems. *In Proceedings of the 2nd International Conference on Service Oriented Computing*, 2004.
15. A. Lazovik, M. Aiello and M. Papazoglou. Associating Assertions with Business Processes and Monitoring their Execution. *In Proceedings of the 2nd International Conference on Service Oriented Computing*, 2004.
16. H. Ludwig, A. Dan, R. Kearney. Cremona: an architecture and library for creation and monitoring of WS-Agreements. In *Proceedings of the Second International Conference on Service Oriented Computing (ICSOC2004)*, New York, NY, USA, 2004.
17. Web Services Agreement Specification (WS-Agreement), 2005. `ws.apache.org/wsif/`.

SENECA – Simulation of Algorithms for the Selection of Web Services for Compositions

Michael C. Jaeger and Gregor Rojec-Goldmann

TU Berlin, Institute of Telecommunication Systems,
Sek. FR 6-10, Franklinstrasse 28/29, D-10587 Berlin, Germany
{mcj, gr}@cs.tu-berlin.de

Abstract. This paper discusses a combinatorial problem about the selection of candidates for Web service compositions. The problem occurs
if we assume that a discovery process has identified several candidates
for each task of a composition and if the selection must consider multiple criteria. We anticipate to use quality-of-service (QoS) categories as
selection criteria and thus the problem is about optimising the QoS of
compositions at their planning-phase. This paper will explain this problem and propose different heuristics as possible solutions. Based on a
software simulation a performance evaluation of these heuristics is given.

1 Introduction

The Web services proposal represents a technology to realise a distributed service
architecture. The basic setup involves a service provider who offers services and a
service requester who invokes the service. The requester finds the desired service
by using a discovery service. The discovery service processes the requirements
from a requester and identifies the suitable available services. Apart from a
functional description, e.g. about the interface, the requester can also define
non-functional characteristics such as the quality of service (QoS) to specify
his requirements. In the Web service domain, an open initiative hosted by the
OASIS group proposes a specification for a discovery service called *Universal
Description, Discovery and Integration*, in short UDDI [17]. The UDDI is a
part of the Web Services Architecture promoted by the W3C [2]. For UDDI,
additional proposals exist that processes the QoS as an additional criteria for
service discovery such as the work of Ran [15] or Benatallah et al. [1].

Individual Web services can be arranged to form a new, composed service.
A software developer can describe such a composition by using flow languages
which exist already for this purpose. Then, execution environments can process
this description to execute the composition. Before, a discovery service must
identify suitable service candidates for each task of the composition. Based on
the result of the discovery, the optimal candidate for each task must be selected.
If the selection must consider more than one criteria, e.g. two QoS categories such
as execution time and cost, then a combinatorial problem arises. In our discussion, we focus entirely on the selection and presume that a preceding discovery

C. Bussler and M.-C. Shan (Eds.): TES 2005, LNCS 3811, pp. 84–97, 2006.

has already identified suitable services. We explain the combinatorial problem of the selection and propose possible solutions. In the following subsections, we give an overview to the QoS of Web services compositions. Then, in Section 2, we explain the problem and introduce possible solutions. In Section 3 we present their evaluation along with a statistical analysis. At the end, the related work is presented and our conclusions are given.

1.1 QoS Categories

We consider the QoS categories as selection criteria. A set of QoS categories has been already introduced for the use with Web services by Zeng et al. [22], or Menasce [12]. From these categories we have chosen the following four to give a more demonstrative discussion and examples. We separate QoS categories by either showing an increasing or a decreasing direction. An increasing direction means that a higher value indicates a better quality, for decreasing categories vice versa. Please note that our methods and algorithms will work also with other and more QoS categories. The considered QoS categories are:

Max. Execution Time (Decreasing). The execution time defines the time to execute the service. We presume that only the execution time values of individual services will result in the overall execution time of the composition.

Cost (Decreasing). The cost defines generally the amount of resources needed to use a service.

Reputation (Increasing). The concept of a reputation is about a ranking given by users of the service. The idea is similar to ebay.com or amazon.com where clients rank the behaviour of other clients [22]. The reputation is defined as the average of the individual ranks of users.

Availability (Increasing). The availability denotes the probability that the execution of the service performs successfully.

1.2 QoS Aggregation

In order to select candidates for tasks in a composition based on QoS, a method is necessary to aggregate the QoS of individual services for the whole composition. In a preceding paper, we have introduced such an aggregation method [9]. The idea of this approach is to map the structure of the composition to fixed structural elements. Then, we perform defined aggregation rules for each structural element and each category. We have derived these structural elements from the workflow patterns introduced by van der Aalst et al. [19]. Workflow patterns describe the functional and structural characteristics of workflow management systems. We have chosen the workflow patterns because van der Aalst has shown that their structural part also applies to commonly known description languages for compositions [18]. Thus, we can presume that our elements cover these descriptions as well. Since the scope of this paper does not allow to explain which of the workflow patterns are considered as a composition element, we would like to refer the reader to our preceding paper [9]. From this analysis, we defined the following composition patterns:

Sequence of service executions. A sequence can either prescribe a specific order in which the services have to be executed or the services can be executed in an arbitrary order.

Loop. The execution of a service or a composition of services is repeated for a certain amount of times.

XOR-split followed by an XOR-join. In a parallel arrangement only one task is started. Thus, the synchronising operation only waits for the started task.

AND-split followed by an AND-join. From a parallel arrangement all tasks are started, and all tasks are required to finish for synchronisation.

AND-split followed by a m-out-of-n-join. From a parallel arrangement all n tasks is started, but less $m < n$ tasks are required to finish for synchronisation.

OR-split followed by OR-join. In a parallel arrangement a subset of the available tasks is started, and all of the started tasks are required to finish for synchronisation. For example, from four available services, the run-time environment starts always three of them which must also finish successfully.

OR-split followed by a m-out-of-n-join. In a parallel arrangement a subset n of all tasks is started, and $m < n$ tasks are required to finish for synchronisation.

Figure 1 shows the pattern-wise aggregation of a simple composition example. To aggregate the maximum execution time, an algorithm would start to determine the larger value in the parallel sub-arrangement. Then, the sum of the sequential arrangement including the aggregated value of the parallel arrangement is calculated. This approach enables us to view the aggregation in a pattern-perspective, i.e. not the whole composition is relevant at once. We have described the aggregation rules for different QoS categories in detail and compared them to other approaches in our preceding paper [9].

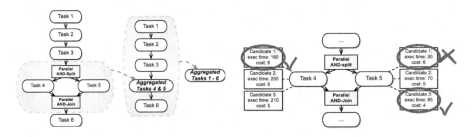

Fig. 1. Collapsing the Graph   **Fig. 2.** Selection Example

2 The Selection of Services

A selection tries to identify the best assignment of service candidates for the tasks in the composition. We propose to use QoS categories as selection criteria. If just one criteria is relevant, the selection is trivial and for each task the referring service candidate offering the best value is chosen. If more than one category is relevant, an algorithm must evaluate all combinations from a global perspective. This need has been discussed already by Zeng et al. [22]. Thus, we give only a small example: consider the parallel arrangement of the two tasks 4 and 5 in Figure 2: let the optimisation goal be to form the quickest composition with the lowest cost. Also, choosing a quicker service is usually more costly meaning that cost and execution time form a trade-off couple. In our example, the quickest candidate for task 4 executes longer than any candidate for task 5. The optimal assignment for the task 5 is the candidate 3. A selection from a local perspective would have identified candidate 1 for task 5 and thus would have resulted in a higher cost.

The problem is that an evaluation of all assignments results in an exponentially rising computation effort regarding the number of candidates: if the number of candidates increases by one, then the number of combinations to evaluate is doubled. Thus, we regard a straightforward evaluation of all combinations as unfeasible for a large number of candidates. Our intention is to apply and evaluate different heuristics for this problem which show a feasible effort.

2.1 Comparing the QoS

All algorithms must compare either the QoS of individual candidates or the aggregated QoS of a composition. For this comparison, we apply the *Simple Additive Weighting (SAW)* method, which was introduced in the context of *Multiple Criteria Decision Making (MCDM)* [7]. For applying the SAW, we refer to a candidate or aggregated set of QoS values with index i and individual QoS values s_{yi}, where y represents a QoS category. Then for each value s_{yi} is replaced by the normalised value n_{yi}:

$$n_{yi} = \begin{cases} \frac{max\{s_{y1},...,s_{yi}\}-s_{yi}}{max\{s_{y1},...,s_{yi}\}-min\{s_{y1},...,s_{yi}\}} & \text{for decreasing categories} \\ \frac{s_{yi}-min\{s_{y1},...,s_{yi}\}}{max\{s_{y1},...,s_{yi}\}-min\{s_{y1},...,s_{yi}\}} & \text{for increasing categories} \end{cases}$$

Then, we apply a score c_i to each candidate which aggregates the normalised values. The score is defined by

$$c_i = \frac{1}{p}\sum_{y=1}^{p} w_y n_{yi}$$

where index p represents the number of considered QoS categories. The weight w_y is applied to the QoS categories by the user's preference. The result of this procedure is a score for each Web service candidate, which can be seen as the value of an item.

2.2 Greedy Selection

A greedy selection represents a simple heuristic approach. This approach selects for each task the candidate that offers the highest score compared to the other candidates. With this approach, it is not possible to consider a constraint which is applied to the whole composition.

2.3 Discarding Subsets

We call our backtracking-based algorithm for the selection *Discarding Subsets*. It uses a search tree which consists of nodes each representing a possible pair of a candidate and a task. Each level of the tree holds pairs of a particular task only, resulting in a tree having the same number of levels as tasks. Each possible assignment for the composition is represented by a path starting from the root and ending at a leaf. The advantage of this algorithm compared to a straight global selection lies in the idea to cut subtrees representing unfavorable combinations to save computation efforts.

Such an approach normally identifies the optimal solution and thus cannot be regarded as an heuristic. However, we regard this as an heuristic, because we establish a cutting rule based on an estimation. Considering the execution time, the cutting rule is clear: if a complete combination has already been determined that shows a lower execution time as the partial combination processed at some moment, the algorithm cuts the subtree. Each additional candidate would worsen execution time. However, for categories where the aggregation calculates the arithmetic mean, a rule cannot determine whether the QoS gets worse or better. In our discussion, we consider the reputation as a QoS category which represents this case. Applied to the selection problem in our configuration, the discarding subsets algorithm considers two cutting rules:

1. A partially evaluated combination already violates a constraint. Thus, the algorithm cuts the subtree.
2. The algorithm compares the aggregated QoS of the partial combination with the aggregated QoS of already complete combinations. However, for this comparison the QoS categories involving a mean-based aggregation are ignored. This strategy does not find the optimal result necessarily, because the cutting rule represents an estimation.

2.4 Bottom-Up Approximation

The selection problem for the composition of Web services shows similarities to the Resource Constrained Project Scheduling Problem (RCSPS) which we have mentioned in a previous publication [8]. An RCPSP occurs in a typical project planning situation: a project is divided into individual tasks. Then, each task must be assigned to the available workers in order to complete the whole project. The problem occurs if the assignment must consider certain optimization or constraint criteria such as finishing the project as quickly as possible. Considering the similarity to the selection problem, an application of solution approaches for RCPSPs sounds feasible. However, not every solution for the RCPSP can be applied to the selection, because RCPSPs cover the execution order of tasks differently: for web service compositions the order is in most cases pre-defined in a flow description, while the tasks of a project are subject to precedence relations, which may allow to push a particular task for- or backwards in order to optimise the utilisation of resources. It turned out that several solutions RCPSPs consider a precedence model which does not allow the application to the selection problem. Nevertheless, we have identified a heuristic covering a RCPSP introduced by Yang et al. which can be used for the selection [20]. The heuristic applied to the selection would perform as follows:

1. The candidates are sorted by the QoS value involving the QoS category relevant for the constraint only.
2. For each task, the algorithm assigns the candidate that offers the best constraint-relevant QoS category. If a solution exists that meets the constraint, it is found with this step.
3. As the next step, the algorithm replaces the firstly assigned candidates by the candidate with the next better QoS score which is determined by applying the SAW method.
4. The new combination is tested for whether the constraint is still kept. If the constraint is still kept, the algorithm continues by looping back to step 3. The algorithm stops, if at one time for each task no additional candidate is found that lets the composition meeting the constraint and increases the overall QoS.

2.5   Pattern-Based Selection

In a preceding paper we have introduced another heuristic [5], which directly covers the example of tasks 4 and 5 explained in section 2. We regret that we cannot go into much detail about the pattern-wise selection due to spatial limitations. Thus, we refer to the mentioned publication for more information. In very brief words, the algorithm determines the best assignment considering each composition pattern in isolation. The algorithm takes advantage of an existing representation of the composition by using the composition patterns. It performs four steps:

1. The algorithm walks recursively into the structure and identifies pattern elements that do not contain any sub-patterns.
2. For all tasks within such an element, all sets of candidate assignments are evaluated. The combination that delivers the best score is chosen.
3. If the optimal solution for a particular pattern is determined, the algorithm walks one level upwards to evaluate the assignment within the new pattern. The aggregated QoS of contained sub-patterns is taken as a fixed value.
4. The pattern wise optimisation and aggregation is performed until the whole composition is covered and one aggregated QoS is returned.

Since this algorithm operates on each pattern element, this approach cannot meet global constraints.

3   Evaluation

We have compared the four proposed heuristics in a software-based evaluation that we call *SENECA*. To the existing four we have also added two simple selection methods to show the optimal result and the result without optimization. The two are: *a*) the *global* selection and the *b*) *constraint* selection. The global selection evaluates all possible combinations and then determines the best assignment possible. This algorithm shows also the worst computation effort. By the second method *b*), the algorithm shows a greedy behaviour: for each individual task, it chooses the candidate offering the best QoS determined by a comparison using the SAW method. To determine an assignment for a task, other assignments the greedy algorithm ignores other assignments and thus the algorithm does not necessarily identify the optimal solution.

In summary, our evaluation covers the following selection methods:

Algorithm *(Respects Constraint)*	
Constraint Selection *(yes)*	Bottom-Up Approach *(yes)*
Global Selection *(no)*	Discarding Subsets *(yes)*
Greedy Selection *(no)*	Pattern-based Selection *(no)*

The evaluation software generates arbitrary test composition structures by randomly arranging the desired number of tasks in composition pattern elements. Since the composition patterns consist of two sequential and five parallel patterns, the generated structures will statistically contain more parallel arrangements. The software performs the following steps:

1. **Creation of the Composition Structure.** To build up the composition structure, the software determines a root pattern chosen from the seven composition elements with uniform probability. Within this root, the software chooses with equal probability to either place a task into it or to choose another composition pattern as a substructure. This ends until the generation has spent the predefined number of tasks. Since the composition patterns consist of two sequential and five parallel patterns, the generated structures will statistically contain more parallel arrangements.

   To our knowledge, the literature does not provide a dedicated evaluation about how many tasks a composition usually consists of. To give an idea about the typical number of services used in the industry, a Gartner study presents the average numbers of (e-)services in companies and enterprises [13]. According to this study small companies deploy about 25 services on average while very large enterprises have a total amount of more than 1000 services. In such very large enterprises, more than 100 clients accessing these services on a regular basis which results in more than one million service executions per day. From these numbers, an estimation is possible that on average a client accesses 10 different services giving on average. This would represent a guess about potential composition sizes used in these environments. The sheer number of 1000 services that must be

Table 1. Availability Rates and Resulting Downtimes by Kenyon [10, p. 411]

System Class	Avalability	Yearly Downtime	Daily Downtime
Unmanaged	90.00000%	876.00 hours	2.40 hours
Managed	99.00000%	87.60 hours	14..40 mins
Well-Managed	99.90000%	8.76 hours	1.44 mins
Fault-Tolerant	99.99000%	52.56 mins	8.64 secs
High-Availability	99.99900%	5.26 mins	863.99 msecs
⋮	⋮	⋮	⋮
Ultra-Availability	99.99999%	3.15 secs	8.64 msecs

considered by a discovery process. However, assumptions about how many services candidates will result for each task cannot be made (except than probably less than 1000).

Besides, there is no known study or evaluation about existing SOA environments and about how many services a composition usually combines. Apart from the Gartner study, such numbers can be guessed from other evaluation work, such as the evaluation of workflow management facilities by Heinis et al. [6] or Cranford et al. [3]. In their work, the underlying number of tasks in workflows varies between 10 and 25.

2. Generation of QoS Values. The software generates candidate services with random QoS values. Regarding the execution time, Tosic et al. have introduced an infrastructure to evaluate the provision of policy-aware Web services [16]. In their work, they have performed experiments to execute Web services while providing an adaptive solution to cover dynamically changes in the given QoS. Their experiments showed that a setup of Web services in a local network resulted in a response time of about 150 milliseconds. Thus, for this work a value of 150 milliseconds is regarded as the quickest service execution possible. Gillmann et al. have evaluated the typical duration for the average turnaround times of activities in a workflow [4]. The workflow scenario represents a real-world application of service compositions. According to their evaluation, automatic (non-interactive) services ususally take about 2 seconds to execute.

Regarding the availability of services, the work of Gillmann et al. considers a typical downtime in the area of 20 minutes each day in their evaluation.[1] This would result in an availability of 0, 985% [4]. Kenyon presents a very detailed discussion about typical availability rates [10, p. 411]. Table 1 summarises typical availability rates.

Regarding the cost and the reputation, an evaluation of existing work would not result in any benefit for this simulation: cost and reputation are individually set and up to specific definitions. For example, the cost depends on the used currency and could be always transferred into another

---

[1] A strongly simplified assumption based on their failure model, which is, however, regarded as sufficient for the use in this work.

measure. For the reputation any scale used for setting scores can be defined. Based on these considerations, the software generates a QoS value – with uniform distribution for execution time, reputation and availability – from the following intervals:

QoS Category, Value Range

Execution Time	$[150..2000]$
Cost	$[0..1000]$
Reputation	$[1..100]$
Availability	$[0,9750..0,9999]$

For the execution time, the actual value for each candidate is determined by adding a randomly determined percentage of between 0 and 100. To form a trade-off couple between execution time and cost, the two are set as follows: the percentage a added to the optimal execution time is taken to calculate the percentage b added to the optimal cost with $a + b = 100$. Thus, the more optimal the execution time is, the worse will be the cost and vice versa.

3. **Setting the Constraint.** After the composition and candidates have been determined, a constraint is set by running the constraint selection first. In our simulations, the cost represents the relevant constraint category. Thus the constraint selection is performed considering the cost. The aggregated cost for the composition is increased by 20% and then taken as the constraint that has to be met by the other selection methods. The resulting QoS of all selection methods are compared with the global selection using the SAW approach. In addition to the resulting QoS also the execution time for each selection method is captured.

4. **Performing the Selection Algorithms.** Having the composition and the candidates with randomly generated QoS attributes, the simulation software performs all selection methods on this setup. For each run, the software captures the resulting aggregated QoS and also the computation time in milliseconds. In addition, the software compares the aggregated QoS of the selection methods resulting by the SAW-based comparison.

We have evaluated the algorithms with arbitrary compositions that contain a different number of tasks (from 4 to 12) but a fixed number of candidates for each task (5). Each evaluation case with a particular number of tasks has been repeated 100 times with each time a new random composition structures and new, randomly generated candidates.

4   Simulation Results

The results are shown in Figures 3 and 4. In addition, Table 2 shows the results from a statistical analysis. Figure 3 shows the average resulting aggregated QoS

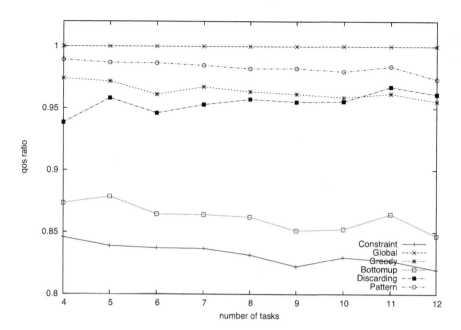

Fig. 3. Relative QoS to Global

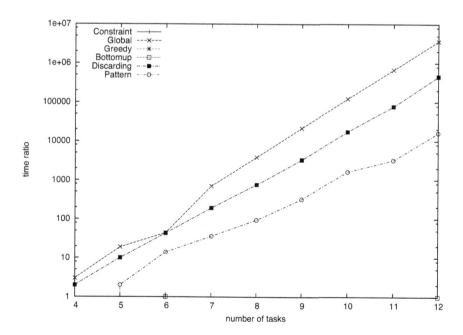

Fig. 4. Computation Times (some of the values remain below 1)

Table 2. Relative QoS and Computation Times for Setup with 12 Tasks

Method	Average Mean $\bar{x}$	Standard Deviation s	% in 1s	% in 2s	% in 3s	95%-Conf. Interval
Overall QoS Relative to Global						
Constraint	0.81961	0.05726	70	95	99	$\pm 0,01122$
Global	1.0	0.0	100	0	0	$\pm 0,00000$
Greedy	0.95539	0.04719	90	96	96	$\pm 0,00924$
Bottom-Up	0.84705	0.05171	66	96	100	$\pm 0,01013$
Discarding Subs.	0.96117	0.04635	87	95	98	$\pm 0,00908$
Pattern	0.97332	0.03590	89	97	98	$\pm 0,00703$
Computation Times (in Milliseconds)						
Constraint	1	0	100	100	100	± 0
Global	3619819	786631	72	95	99	$\pm 154.179,676$
Greedy	1	0	100	100	100	± 0
Bottom-Up	1	5	92	92	95	$\pm 0,98$
Discarding Subs.	452854	741794	89	94	96	$\pm 0,00703$
Pattern	16061	82974	97	99	99	$[-16060; +16262]$

of the compositions performing the selection methods relative to the global selection. For example, a QoS ratio of $0,80$ means that this selection method gains on average 80% of the best QoS possible. Figure 4 shows the average execution times of the different selection methods for compositions with increasing number of tasks. Please note that in both figures the discrete results are connected with interpolated lines for better visualisation only. Table 2 lists the arithmetic mean and the standard deviation s based on the 100 samples taken. Based on the standard deviation, the table also shows how many percent of the samples are within one, two or three standard deviations around the mean.

4.1 Analysis

From the results in Table 2 we can guess that the resulting aggregated QoS ranges around the mean value. Thus, we can exclude a split performance in the way that they either perform very well or very badly. Furthermore, we can derive the following observations:

Constraint. This method represents the lower limit regarding the resulting QoS. It shows that theoretically the optimal solution increases the given setup by roughly 25%.

Global. The global selection results in the optimal overall QoS while ignoring the constraint. It shows exponentially rising computation effort with a larger number of candidates and thus cannot be regarded as a feasible solution.

Greedy. The greedy selection shows that about 95% of the samples (assuming an error rate of 5% in our simulation) result in a QoS at least better that about 86% of the optimal QoS. We see also that the computational effort is negligible.

However, it cannot meet any given constraints on purpose. Considering that about 80% of the samples result within one standard deviation, we can conclude that the greedy selection results in around 95% of the optimal Quality.

Bottom-up. The Bottom-up selection results in the second worse QoS compared to the other heuristics. However, it meets the constraint and also shows a negligible computational effort.

Discarding. The selection by discarding subsets results in the best QoS possible while still meeting the constraint. The measurements show that 95% of the samples result in about 87% of the optimal QoS. Considering the result from the constraint selection, this method increases on average the aggregated QoS by 15%. Its computational effort is roughly one eighth of the global selection, however it raises still exponentially.

Pattern. The pattern based selection shows the best resulting QoS from all heuristic approaches. It also shows the lowest deviation of the resulting QoS. We regard the computational effort as reasonable, thus it can be considered as an alternative compared to the greedy selection. This method seems to depend strongly on the given composition structure, because it shows the largest deviation of execution times.

5 Related Work

The work of Puschner and Schedel about calculating the execution time for software architectures represents our foundation for the aggregation of QoS in Web service compositions [14]. They have defined calculation rules for structural patterns as found in software executions. Since our composition model plays in the field of Web service compositions, we have adopted this principle and build our patterns onto the workflow patterns by van der Aalst et al. [19].

Several authors have also discussed which QoS categories might be considered in Web service compositions [12] [22]. Their contribution has been taken up to determine the relevant categories for our work. Using QoS statements as the main criteria for the selection of Web services has been discussed by different works already [1] [15]. Zeng et al. [22] already discussed the selection of candidates as a part of a framework for Web service compositions in general where our contribution about comparing different heuristics for the selection problem would represent a suitable supplement. Apart from the selection, Zeng et al. propose different aggregation mechanisms for each of their considered QoS categories. Also, there are some more contributions about selection algorithms, such as the work of Lee [11] or Yu et al. [21], in which the selection of services is compared to a variant of the knapsack problem. We think that because of its uniform structure, the pattern-wise aggregation results in lower efforts for the implementation and the computation of the aggregation while being more independent from particular QoS categories.

6   Conclusions

We have discussed different algorithms for performing the selection of candidates to optimise the aggregated QoS of a composition. Considering the algorithms, the selected QoS categories can be extended depending on what is considered for a specific application case. The intention of our work is to focus on the selection algorithms independent from particular QoS categories.

For the optimisation *without* the need to meet a constraint, the pattern-based selection reaches almost the level of the best possible QoS with acceptable computational effort. If a slight decrease of the overall QoS is tolerable (up to approximately 15% percent of the optimal solution by our setup), the greedy selection delivers acceptable results with negligible efforts. For the optimisation *with* meeting a global constraint, the bottom-up approximation results in an overall QoS about 10% worse than by using the discarding subsets approach while showing negligible computational efforts with growing number of candidates.

The results show that for a selection in a time-critical scenario, heuristics can be successfully applied with a low decrease of the aggregated QoS. For future research in this direction possible test cases could operate on a fixed composition structure with an increasing number of candidates to evaluate the different algorithms with specific arrangements. We also plan to evaluate how the performance of the heuristics depend on the variance of the given QoS values of the individual candidates.

References

1. Boualem Benatallah, Marlon Dumas, Marie-Christine Fauvet, and Fethi A. Rabhi. Towards Patterns of Web Services Composition. Technical Report UNSW-CSE-TR-0111, University of New South Wales, 2001.
2. David Booth, Hugo Haas, Francis McCabe, Eric Newcomer, Michael Champion, Chris Ferris, and David Orchard. Web Services Architecture. http://www.w3.org/TR/ws-arch/, February 2004.
3. Jonathan Cranford, Ravi Mukkamala, and Vijayalakshmi Atluri. Modeling and evaluation of distributed workflow algorithms. In *Proceedings of the World Multiconference on Systemics, Cybernetics and Informatics: Information Systems Development*, pages 183–188, Orlando, Florida, USA, July 2001. IIIS.
4. Michael Gillmann, Gerhard Weikum, and Wolfgang Wonner. Workflow Management with Service Quality Guarantees. In *Proceedings of the 2002 ACM SIGMOD International Conference on Management of Data*, pages 228–239, Madison, Wisconsin, USA, June 2002. ACM Press.
5. Roy Grønmo and Michael C. Jaeger. Model-Driven Methodology for Building QoS-Optimised Web Service Compositions. In *Proceedings of the 5th IFIP International Conference on Distributed Applications and Interoperable Systems (DAIS'05)*, pages 68–82, Athens, Greece, May 2005. Springer Press.
6. Thomas Heinis, Cesare Pautasso, and Gustavo Alonso. Design and evaluation of an autonomic workflow engine. In *Proceedings of the Second International Conference on Autonomic Computing (ICAC'05)*, pages 27–38, Seattle, Washington, USA, June 2005. IEEE Press.

7. Ching-Lai Hwang and K. Paul Yoon, editors. *Multiple Attribute Decision Making: Methods and Applications*, volume 186 of *Lecture Notes in Economics and Mathematical Systems*. Springer-Verlag, March 1981.
8. Michael C. Jaeger, Gero Mühl, and Sebastian Golze. QoS-aware Composition of Web Services: A Look at Selection Algorithms. In *Proceedings of the 3rd International Conference on Web Services (ICWS 2005)*, Orlando, Florida, USA, July 2005.
9. Michael C. Jaeger, Gregor Rojec-Goldmann, and Gero Mühl. QoS Aggregation for Service Composition using Workflow Patterns. In *Proceedings of the 8th International Enterprise Distributed Object Computing Conference (EDOC'04)*, pages 149–159, Monterey, California, September 2004. IEEE Press.
10. Tony Kenyon. *Data Networks: Routing, Seurity, and Performance Optimization*. Digital Press, 1st edition edition, June 15th 2002.
11. Juhnyoung Lee. Matching Algorithms for Composing Business Process Solutions with Web Services. In *Proceedings of the 4th International Conference on E-Commerce and Web Technologies (ECWEB 03)*, pages 393–402, Prague, CZ, October 2003. Springer-Verlag Heidelberg.
12. Daniel A. Menasce. QoS Issues in Web Services. In *IEEE Internet Computing*, pages 72–75. IEEE Press, November-December 2002.
13. Massimo Pezzini. SOA Beyond Hype and Disillusionment – A Strategic Perspective. Key Note given at the SOA Days 2005 Technology Conference, September 2005.
14. Peter Puschner and Anton Schedl. Computing Maximum Task Execution Times - A Graph-Based Approach. *Journal of Real-Time Systems*, 13(1):67–91, July 1997.
15. Shuping Ran. A model for web services discovery with QoS. *SIGecom Exch.*, 4(1):1–10, 2003.
16. Vladimir Tosic, Wei Ma, Bernard Pagurek, and Babak Esfandiari. Web service offerings infrastructure (wsoi) – a management infrastructure for xml web services. In *Proceedings of the IEEE/IFIP Network Operations and Management Symposium (NOMS'04)*, pages 817–830, Seoul, South Korea, April 2004. IEEE Press.
17. UDDI Spec Technical Committee. UDDI Version 3.0.1. http://uddi.org/pubs/uddi-v3.0.1-20031014.pdf, 2003.
18. Wil M.P. van der Aalst. Don't go with the flow: Web services composition standards exposed. *Jan/Feb 2003 Issue of IEEE Intelligent Systems*, pages 72–76, January 2003.
19. Wil M.P. van der Aalst and Arthur H.M. ter Hofstede and B. Kiepuszewski and A.P. Barros. Workflow Patterns. *Distributed and Parallel Databases 14(3)*, pages 5–51, 2003.
20. Bibo Yang, Joseph Geunes, and William J. O'Brien. Resource Constrained Project Scheduling; Past Work and New Directions. Technical Report Research Report 2001-6, Department of Industrial and Systems Engineering, University of Florida, 2001.
21. Tao Yu and Kwei-Jay Lin. Service selection algorithms for web services with end-to-end qos constraints. In *Proceedings of the 2005 IEEE International Conference on e-Technology, e-Commerce and e-Service (EEE'05)*, pages 129–136, Hong Kong, China, March 2005. IEEE Press.
22. Liangzhao Zeng, Boualem Benatallah, Anne H.H. Ngu, Marlon Dumas, Jayant Kalagnanam, and Henry Chang. QoS-Aware Middleware for Web Services Composition. *IEEE Transactions on Software Transactions*, 30(5):311–327, May 2004.

Monitoring for Hierarchical Web Services Compositions[*]

Debmalya Biswas and Krishnamurthy Vidyasankar

Dept. of Computer Science, Memorial University of Newfoundland,
St. John's, NL, Canada A1B 3X5
{debmalya, vidya}@cs.mun.ca

Abstract. The most promising feature of the Web services platform is its ability to form new services by combining the capabilities of already existing services, i.e., its composability. The existing services may themselves be composed of other services, leading to a hierarchical composition. In this work, we focus on the monitoring aspect for hierarchical Web services compositions. We are primarily interested in capturing the state of a hierarchical composition at any given point of time (snapshot). We discuss in detail how some of the snapshot algorithms proposed in literature can be extended in a Web services context. Snapshots usually reflect a state of the system which "might have occurred". Towards this end, we show how we can acquire a state that "actually occurred" from such snapshots. Finally, we discuss the different types of execution related queries and how we can answer them using the captured snapshots.

1 Introduction

Industry and researchers acknowledge Web services as being at the heart of next generation distributed systems. The most promising aspect of the Web services platform is the composability aspect, i.e., its ability to form new services by combining the capabilities of already existing services. Basically, there are two approaches to composing a service: dynamic and static. In the dynamic approach, given a complex user request, the system comes up with a plan to fulfill the request depending on the capabilities of available Web services at run-time. In the static approach, given a set of Web services, composite services are defined manually at design-time combining their capabilities. In this paper, we consider a mix of the two approaches where the composite services are defined statically but the binding with providers is performed at run-time depending on the user request. The above approach is typical of a group of organizations collaborating to provide recurring, general services usually requested by users. Thus, we assume that the organizations (providers) agree on some of the compositional aspects such as the ontology model used to describe their services, log syntax, underlying state transition model, etc.

Monitoring is an inherent requirement of any distributed system. The need for a monitoring mechanism is even more critical for Web services compositions because

---

[*] This research is supported in part by the Natural Sciences and Engineering Research Council of Canada Discovery Grant 3182.

C. Bussler and M.-C. Shan (Eds.): TES 2005, LNCS 3811, pp. 98–112, 2006.

of their complexity and long running nature. OWL-S states the need for execution monitoring as "the ability to find out where in the process the request is and whether any unanticipated glitches have appeared". In this work, we only consider the first part, i.e., providing information about the current state of the execution. Monitoring Web services compositions, similar to distributed systems, is difficult because of the following reasons:

- No global observer: Due to their distributed nature, we cannot assume the existence of an entity having visibility over the entire composition. In fact, due to their privacy and autonomy requirements, even the composite service provider may not have visibility over the internal processing of its component service providers.
- Non-determinism: Web services allow parallel composition of processes. Also, Web services usually depend on external factors for their execution. As such, it may not be possible to predict their behavior before the actual execution. For example, whether a flight booking will succeed or not depends on the number of available seats (at the time of booking) and cannot be predicted in advance.
- Unpredictable communication delays: Communication delays make it impossible to record the states of all the involved providers instantaneously. For example, let us assume that provider A initiates an attempt to record the state of the composition. Then, by the time the request (to record its state) reaches provider B and B records its state, provider A's state might have changed.
- Dynamic configuration: The service providers are selected incrementally as the execution progresses (dynamic binding). Thus, the "components" of the distributed system may not be known in advance.

The services invoked by a composite service may themselves be composite, leading to a hierarchical composition. We refer to the service (provider) invoking another service (provider) to execute part of its functionality as the parent and child services (providers) respectively. The definitions of ancestor and descendent providers in a hierarchical composition follow analogously. We are primarily interested in capturing the state of a hierarchical Web services composition at any given point of time. The problem of "capturing the state of a system" has been studied extensively in the area of Distributed Systems and the solutions are usually categorized as snapshot algorithms. We discuss in detail how some of the snapshot algorithms proposed in literature can be adapted to capture snapshots of hierarchical Web services compositions. Snapshots usually reflect a state of the system which "might have occurred". Snapshot algorithms capable of capturing a state that "actually occurred" usually assume synchronized clocks [M91], [L78], [M89] or real-time timestamps [B04]. Towards this end, we show how we can acquire an actual state of the composition without the above assumptions. Finally, we discuss the different types of execution related queries and how we can answer them using the captured snapshots.

The rest of the paper is organized as follows: Section 2 introduces the underlying state transition and composition model. Section 3 provides a detailed discussion about the "state" of a hierarchical composition beginning with algorithms to capture the state to how the captured information can be utilized. Section 4 concludes the work and provides directions for future work.

2 State Transition and Web Services Composition Model

We assume the existence of a coordinator and log manager corresponding to each
provider as shown in Fig. 1. The coordinator is responsible for all non-functional aspects related to the execution of the provider such as monitoring, transactions, etc.
The log manager logs information about any state transitions as well as any messages
sent/received by the provider. The state transitions and messages considered are as
outlined in Fig.2:

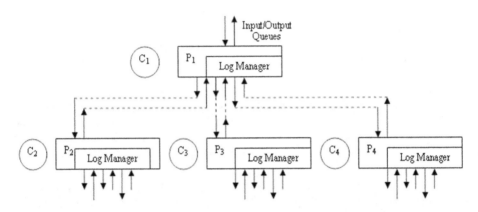

Fig. 1. Composition infrastructure

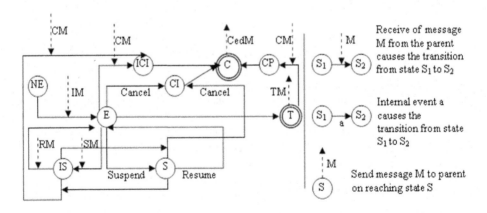

Fig. 2. Provider life cycle

- Not - Executing (NE): The provider is waiting for an invocation.
- Executing (E): On receiving an Invocation message (IM), the provider changes its
  state from NE to E.
- Suspended (S) and Suspended by Invoker (IS): A provider, in state E, may change
  its state to S due to an internal event (Suspend) or to IS on the receipt of a Suspend

message (SM). Conversely, the transition from S to E occurs due to an internal event (Resume) and from IS to E on receiving a Resume message (RM).

– Canceling (CI), Canceling due to invoker (ICI) and Canceled (C): A provider, in state E/S/IS, may change its state to CI due to an internal event (Cancel) or ICI on the receipt of a Cancel message (CM). Once it finishes cancellation, it changes its state to C and sends a Canceled message (CedM) to its parent. Please note that cancellation may require canceling the effects of some of its children.

– Terminated (T) and Compensating (CP): The provider changes its state to T once it has finished executing the operation. On termination, the provider sends a Terminated message (TM) to its parent. A provider may be required to cancel an operation even after it has finished executing the operation (compensation). A provider, in state T, changes its state to CP on receiving the CM. Once it finishes compensation, it moves to C and sends a CedM to its parent.

To keep the discussion simple, we assume that each provider is responsible for executing a single operation (composite/primitive). The state of a provider at time t is its execution history till t. For simplicity (and where there is no scope for confusion), we represent the state of a provider at t in terms of the state of its executing operation at t and, sometimes, also as a combination of the states of its executing and invoked operations at t. For example, if the execution history of a provider P_A till t is "(Receive IM of a_1 from User, E_1) (E_{11}, Send IM of a_{11} to P_B) (E_{12}, Send IM of a_{12} to P_C) (Receive TM of a_{11} from P_B, T_{11})" then the state of P_A at t can be represented as E_1 or E_1 (T_{11}, E_{12}).

In a hierarchical composition, the lifecycles of a parent and child provider are not independent. In fact, the discussion till now (Fig. 2) can be considered as the lifecycle of a child provider with respect to its parent. Fig. 3 shows the lifecycle stages of a parent with respect to one of its children. The same cycle would be repeated for other children. We discuss the lifecycle stages with the help of an example scenario where a composite provider P invokes an operation a_{11} of provider Q.

– Normal execution: Once P starts executing an operation (E), it is capable of invoking operations of other providers. To invoke operation a_{11}, P sends the corresponding IM to Q.

– Suspension: Provider P may decide to suspend any of its invoked operations (which are still executing). For example, if P is currently in state E_1 (E_{11}) and it decides to suspend the operation a_{11} then it sends the corresponding SM to Q and changes its state to E_1 (IS_{11}). Whenever P decides to resume operation a_{11}, it sends the corresponding RM to Q and changes its state back to E_1 (E_{11}).

– Cancellation: We allow for two types of cancellation. (1) Provider P decides to cancel one of its invoked operations. For example, if P is currently in state E_1 (E_{11}) or E_1 (T_{11}) and it decides to cancel the operation a_{11} then it sends the corresponding CM to Q and changes its state to E_1 (ICI_{11}) or E_1 (CP_{11}) accordingly. Please note that the same message CM is used for both cancellation and compensation. We do not differentiate between the two because of synchronization problems between parent-child providers. To illustrate the problem, let us assume that we have separate messages for cancellation (CM) and compensation (say, CpM). Consider a situation where the child has terminated (T) but its TM has not yet reached the parent. Now, if the parent had to cancel the execution of the child, it would send a CM to the child (since the state of the child is still E at the parent's site). However, the child has already terminated and requires a CpM to cancel its effects. (2) Provider P needs to cancel its execution (due to an internal event Cancel or on receiving the CM from its parent), implying cancellation for all the operations invoked by P. For example, if the current state of P is E_1 (T_{11}) and it receives a CM then it sends a CM to Q and changes its state to ICI_1 (CP_{11}). Please note that the above state transition is not evident from Fig. 3.

- Termination: Provider P changes the state of a_{11} to T (C) on receiving the TM (CedM) from Q. Needless to say, P can change the state of its operation a_1 to T (C) only after it has received the TM (CedM) from the providers of all the operations invoked by P.

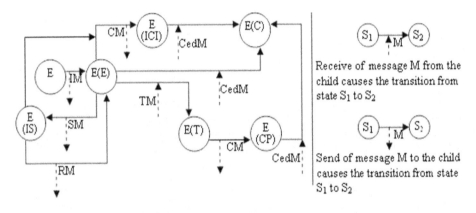

Fig. 3. Parent provider life cycle (with respect to one of its children)

We assume that the composition schema (static composition) specifies a partial order for the operations invoked by a provider. We define the happened-before relation between the operations invoked by a provider as follows:

An operation a *happened-before* operation b invoked by the same provider (a --> b) if and only if one of the following holds: (1) There exists a control/data dependency between operations a and b such that a needs to terminate before b can start executing. (2) There exists an operation c invoked by the same provider such that a --> c and c --> b.

An operation, on failure, is retried with the same or different providers till it completes successfully (terminates). Note that each (retrial) attempt is considered as a new invocation and would be logged accordingly. Finally, to accommodate asynchronous communication, we assume the presence of Input/Output (I/O) queues. Basically, each provider has an I/O queue with respect to its parent and children as shown in Fig. 1. The Input (Output) queue of a provider P corresponding to provider Q is referred to as I_{PQ} (O_{PQ}). We assume that the status of the I/O queues and logs are updated in an atomic manner. With respect to Fig. 2 and Fig. 3, for any message M whose send (receive) causes the provider to change its state, the details of the state transition are written to the log and M inserted into (deleted from) the Output (Input) queue in an atomic fashion. For example, as soon as an operation terminates, the state of the operation in the log is updated to T and the corresponding TM inserted into the Output queue atomically.

3 State of the Composition

3.1 Background

Research in the area of Web services monitoring [PBBST04], [LAP03] has focused on monitoring as a mechanism for detecting and handling failures. [PBBST04] uses monitoring to detect and signal if the invoked providers are behaving according to the specified protocols. In [LAP03], the monitor is responsible for the entire execution process starting from requesting the planner to come up with a plan for the user request to ensuring that the execution is proceeding as per plan (once execution starts).

The problem of "capturing the state of a system" has been studied extensively in the area of Distributed Systems. A distributed system is usually modeled as a graph whose vertices and edges represent the nodes and the bi-directional communication channels connecting the nodes respectively. If we can freeze the computation at some instant t, the snapshot would consist of the node states and the contents of the channels at t. The contents of a channel are the messages sent, but not yet received, by the nodes on that channel. However, freezing the execution may not always be possible (and even if possible should be avoided). Snapshot algorithms try to record the node states and channel contents in such a way that they form a complete and consistent state of the system. Consistency is usually defined by the condition "if the receive event of a message has been recorded in the state of a node then the corresponding send event should also have been recorded".

3.2 Synchronized Clock Snapshot Algorithm

In this section, we discuss snapshot algorithms based on the assumption that the clocks of the providers are synchronized. The absence of perfectly synchronized clocks in a distributed setting has been studied extensively by researchers. Several clock synchronization protocols have been proposed based on the notion of logical [L78], [M89] and physical [M91] clocks. In [L78], Lamport presents an algorithm to partially order the events across the system based on the assumption that the clocks are monotonically increasing. An interesting property (or limitation) of Lamport's algorithm is: "If event a happened before event b then $T(a) < T(b)$ (where $T(a)$ and $T(b)$ are the timestamps associated with events a and b respectively). However, if $T(x) < T(y)$, it is not possible to determine if event x causally happened-before y or if they are concurrent". [M89] overcomes the above limitation by attaching vector timestamps to the events. Basically, it ensures that the timestamps of two concurrent events are incomparable. Network Time Protocol (NTP) [M91] extends clock synchronization for large networks connected over the internet. NTP provides skews in the range of 1-30 ms, even for wide area networks. NTP is based on physically synchronizing the clocks in a distributed system with an external clock such as a GPS clock or other radio clocks. However, the above approaches require considerable coordination among the participants (providers), which may not always be possible in a Web services scenario due to the autonomy of the providers. A more loosely coupled approach for clock synchronization is the use of a timestamp element as advocated by WS standards like WS-Security [WSA] for SOAP messages. Basically, a timestamp element consists of the creation time and transmission delays. Given this, we can calculate the skew (drift) between the parent and child providers' clocks as follows: *skew*

= (receiver's processing time - sender's creation time - transmission delay). Although the synchronization achieved with message timestamps may not be as accurate as with NTP, we believe that it would still be acceptable for most Web services scenarios given their long-lived nature.

Given synchronized clocks and logging (as discussed earlier), a snapshot of the hierarchical composition at time t would consist of the logs of all the "relevant" providers till time t (hereafter, the log of a provider P till time t is referred to as log_{Pt}). The relevant providers can be determined in a recursive manner (starting from the root provider) by considering the providers of the invoked operations recorded in the parent provider's log till time t. If message timestamps are used then we need to consider the skew while recording the logs, i.e., if a parent provider's log was recorded till time t then its children providers' logs need to be recorded till (t + skew). The states of the I/O queues can be determined from the state transition model. For example, if for a pair of parent (P) - child (Q) providers, log_{Pt} denotes the state of an operation a_t as E while log_{Qt} denotes its state as T/C then add the TM/CedM corresponding to a_t to I_{PQ}.

3.3   Distributed Snapshot Algorithm for Web Services (DSW)

In this section, we do not assume synchronized clocks and outline an extension of the Distributed Snapshots Algorithm (DSA) [CL85] to capture the state of a composition. Before describing the extension, let us take a brief look at the original DSA. DSA requires the channels to preserve the FIFO property. In addition to the messages belonging to the underlying computation, the DSA assumes a special type of message called markers. The markers do not have any effect on the underlying computation. The algorithm can be initiated by one or more processes, each of which records its state, without receiving markers from other processes. The DSA can be divided into two phases: 1) the recording phase and 2) the collection phase. The recording mechanism given by [CL85] is as follows:

Marker-Sending Rule for a Process p. For each channel c, incident on, and directed away from p:

   p sends one marker along c after p records its state and before p sends further messages along c.

Marker-Receiving Rule for a Process q. On receiving a marker along a channel c:

   if q has not recorded its state then
      begin q records its state
         q records the state c as the empty sequence
      end
   else q records the state of c as the sequence of messages received along c after q's state was recorded and before q received the marker along c.   □

Once the states have been recorded by all the nodes (the recording phase has terminated), they need to be collected to get a snapshot of the system. The collection phase is context dependant and [CL85] does not give any specific mechanisms to collect the recorded states. For example, all the nodes may send their recorded states to a previously agreed upon node or flood the recorded states through the system so that each node can determine the snapshot of the system.

Distributed Snapshot algorithm for Web services (DSW):

Assumption: The I/O queues maintain the FIFO order of the messages.

The algorithm is initiated by the root provider, which atomically records its state (as of the time of recording) and sends markers to its children providers. By recording its state at time t, we mean that a provider records the contents of its local log at t, i.e., its execution history till t.

Child providers, on receiving the markers, do the same, i.e., atomically record their states (as of the time of recording) and send markers to their children providers. This downward propagation of the markers continues till leaf providers are reached.

The states of the I/O queues are computed as outlined for the synchronized clock scenario.   □

The above algorithm (DSW) differs from the original DSA as follows:

- In DSA, markers are sent along all the outgoing channels. Basically, DSA assumes that the network topology is static (fixed in advance). With Web services compositions, due to dynamic binding, a provider at any point of time is only aware of the providers of the operations it has invoked till then. A provider may invoke other providers after it has recorded its state. Thus, the set of providers, whose states are recorded, may vary from one snapshot to the next.
- Our algorithm does not require the providers to record the states of their I/O queues explicitly. The contents of the I/O queues can be determined from the local states of the providers as discussed earlier.

Correctness: As with the DSA, here also we show that the above algorithm captures a state of the hierarchical composition which "might have occurred" (is consistent with the state transitions discussed earlier). More precisely, we show that the recorded states preserve the causality of the messages sent/received, i.e., if the reception of a message is recorded then its transmission has also been recorded. Intuitively, the proof follows from the fact that messages are exchanged only between parent-child providers and that the state of a parent is always recorded before any of its children. Thus,

- for messages recorded as received by any parent: If the receive event is recorded, then its corresponding send event (by the child) will also get recorded as the state of the child is recorded later.
- for messages recorded as received by any child: The FIFO nature of the I/O queues ensures that the parent sent the corresponding message before sending the marker. And, since the recording of state and sending of markers is done in an atomic fashion, the corresponding send event would have been recorded by the parent.   □

DSW captures the state of the hierarchical composition till the lowest level (leaf providers). The algorithm can be customized as follows to record the state of the composition up to a certain granularity:

- Capture the state up to level n: Append a counter with the marker. Each child provider, on receiving the marker, increments the counter by 1 and forwards it to its children (if any) if the value of the counter <= n.

– Capture the state till a certain condition holds: The condition may be time based (for example, capture the states of as many providers as possible within a time frame) or any predicate which can be evaluated locally. Similar to the above case, we can accommodate this requirement by appending the predicate to the marker, i.e., a provider forwards the received marker to only those children for which the attached predicate evaluates to true.

Snapshot algorithms are primarily used to capture an intermediate state of the execution. As such there might be a need to run it multiple times for the same execution. However, we cannot apply the idea of incremental snapshots [V89] directly here. A provider cannot decide to forward the marker to only those children to (from) which it has sent (received) messages after the last snapshot. Although the provider may not have exchanged any messages with its children since the last snapshot, the state of the lower level providers may have changed. Exceptions include scenarios where the children providers have either terminated or canceled. While terminated lower level child providers may be canceled (compensation), it would involve the send of a CM (a provider cannot decide to compensate itself). Even without the idea of incremental snapshots, it may not be required to traverse the entire hierarchy for each snapshot. A provider P may proactively take snapshots of the subtree rooted at P. On receiving the marker, P checks if the latest recorded snapshot (of the subtree rooted at P) is consistent. If so, there is no need to forward the marker to P's children. The snapshot is consistent if and only if the recorded states of P and its parent are consistent with the earlier state transition discussion. For example, if the state of an operation a_i is recorded as T at the parent provider's site (P's parent) then a_i's recorded state should be T at the child provider's (P's) site too.

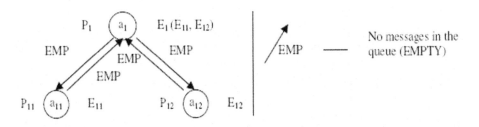

Fig. 4. Sample Snapshot showing "what might have occurred"

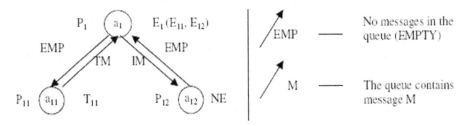

Fig. 5. Execution showing what "might have actually occurred"

3.4   Actual State of the Composition

As mentioned earlier, the snapshot acquired by the DSW highlights a global state of the composition which "might have occurred". For example, let us consider a single-level composition. Now the algorithm might record the states of the providers in the composition as shown in Fig. 4 namely, that operations a_1, a_{11} and a_{12} are all executing. However, the execution might have happened as shown in Fig. 5 where operation a_{11} had terminated before a_{12} started executing, i.e., operations a_{11} and a_{12} were never executing simultaneously.

Let P_S denote the set of providers whose states were recorded as part of a DSW snapshot S. For a pair of parent-child providers in P_S, if the state of the parent was recorded at time t then the child's state would have been recorded at a later time (t + L). Thus, the providers in P_S may never have been in their recorded states simultaneously. We can still infer the following about the states of the providers in P_S at t based on the state of a provider P in P_S recorded at t.

- The presence of an operation a_t in the recorded state of P implies that all the operations having a happened-before relation with a_t have terminated by t (their states are T at t).
- If the recorded state of P is E/S/IS/CI/ICI then its ancestors cannot be in the states T/CP/C at t.
- If the recorded state of P is T(C) then all the providers in the sub-tree rooted at P are in the state T (C) at t.

We use the above observations to acquire a state of the composition which "actually occurred". We define an actual state of the composition as follows:

A global state represents the actual state of the composition at time t if it reflects the states at t of all and only those providers invoked till t.

The concept of actual states is similar to the notion of Strongly Consistent Global States (SCGS) [B04] in literature. While [B04] defines SCGS in terms of the local states of all the providers in the system, we define the actual state at a time t in terms of the local states of the providers invoked till t (due to dynamic binding). Algorithms to detect SCGS in [B04] are based on real-time timestamps (similar to our algorithm based on synchronized clocks).

Given a (DSW) snapshot S initiated at time t, we can acquire an actual state of the composition at some point t_p in the past ($t_p <= t$) as given below:

Actual State Algorithm: /* Intuitively, we can simulate "freezing the execution" if we can determine a time t_p at which none of the providers invoked until that time are executing, i.e., they are in the state T/C at t_p. Thus, the algorithm tries to determine the latest set of providers which have definitely been canceled or terminated till t. The algorithm achieves this by determining the most recent time t_p when all the children providers at the root level are in the states T/C (implying all the lower level providers invoked till t_p are also in the states T/C). We illustrate the steps with the help of an example scenario (Fig. 6 and 7). Fig. 6 depicts a sample DSW snapshot (only shows the current states of the recorded operations), Fig. 7 shows the recorded state of the root provider (contents of its log till t).*/

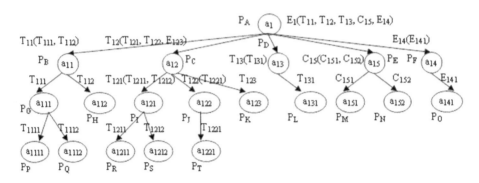

Fig. 6. Sample DSW snapshot S

(Receive IM of a_1 from User, E_1)(E_{11}, Send IM of a_{11} to P_B)(Receive TM of a_{11} from P_B, T_{11})

(E_{12}, Send IM of a_{12} to P_C)(Receive TM of a_{12} from P_C, T_{12})(E_{13}, Send IM of a_{13} to P_D)(E_{15},

Send IM of a_{15} to P_E)(Receive TM of a_{13} from P_D, T_{13})(Receive TM of a_{15} from P_E, T_{15})

(E_{114}, Send IM of a_{14} to P_F)(CP_{15}, Send CM of a_{15} to P_E)(Receive CedM of a_{15} from P_E, C_{15})

t_p t

Fig. 7. Recorded state of the root provider

1. Let P_{IN} denote the set of invoked providers in the recorded state of the root provider. If the state of each provider P in P_{IN} is either C/T then terminate the algorithm /* the recorded snapshot represents an actual state of the composition */.

2. From the recorded state of the root provider, determine the last provider P_l in P_{IN} to terminate/cancel before the invocation of the first provider P_f in P_{IN} which is still executing (in state E/IS/ICI) /* the "last" part (of the above statement) helps us in acquiring the latest set while the "first" part ensures that the acquired set consists only of terminated/canceled providers. $P_{IN} = \{P_B, P_C, P_D, P_E, P_F\}$, $P_l = P_E$ and $P_f = P_F$ */. *Given this, t_p corresponds to the time just after P_l terminated/canceled.*

/* The following steps determine the providers invoked (at all levels) till t_p and their states at t_p. Recall that the recorded states of the providers reflect their states at a later time t. As discussed earlier, the states of all the providers (invoked till t_p) would be C/T at t_p. A small complication arises due to the possibility of compensation. A provider which was in state T at t_p may have been compensated before t (after t_p) leading to its state being recorded as C. For example, the recorded state of the provider P_E is C (Fig. 6). However, from the log (Fig. 7) it is clear that the state of P_E was T at t_p. As such, we may need to adjust the recorded states of some of the providers (invoked till t_p) so that they reflect their states at t_p. */

3. Let S_{AP} denote the set of invoked providers (at all levels) till t_p. Initially, $S_{AP} = $ Root provider.

4. Adjust the recorded state of the root provider so that it reflects its state at t_p (contents of its log till t_p - Fig. 7). Use the newly adjusted state to determine the set of providers P_{TP} invoked by the root provider (its children) till t_p and their states at t_p. Adjust the recoded states of providers in P_{TP} accordingly (if required). Add the providers in P_{TP} to S_{AP}, i.e., $S_{AP} = S_{AP} \cup P_{TP}$ /* the adjusted recorded state of the root provider denotes the state of P_E as T, so adjust the recorded state of P_E accordingly (trim its log till t_p - Fig. 8) */.
5. Repeat Step 4 recursively for each provider in P_{TP} (determined at each stage) till leaf providers are reached. /* $S_{AP} = \{P_A, P_B, P_C, P_D, P_E, P_G, P_H, P_I, P_J, P_K, P_L, P_M, P_N, P_P, P_Q, P_R, P_S, P_T\}$ */

The global state G, consisting of the states of the providers in S_{AP}, represents the actual state of the composition at time t_p - Fig. 9.

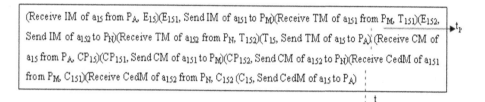

Fig. 8. Recorded state of the provider P_E

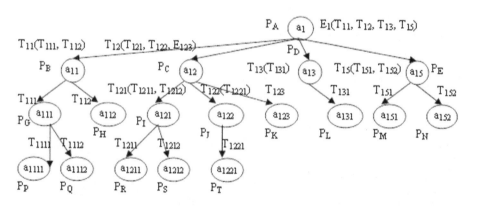

Fig. 9. Actual state corresponding to the snapshot in Fig. 6

It is easy to observe that the above mechanism can be used to acquire an actual state for any sub-tree belonging to a snapshot acquired by the DSW. For example, if we add another level of nesting to the composition in Fig. 6 (Fig. 10) then the above mechanism can be used to acquire an actual state for the sub-tree rooted at P_A.

3.5 Answering Execution Status Related Queries

Sometimes a diagram representing the state of the entire composition may contain too much information to comprehend. As such, it should be possible to answer specific queries related to the state of execution. We discuss the capabilities and limitations of the different snapshots (acquired using the algorithms mentioned earlier) with respect to answering different types of queries. We divide the queries into the following categories:

- Local queries: Queries which can be answered based on the local state information of a provider. For example, queries such as "What is the current state of provider P?" or "Has P reached a specific state?". As obvious, we do not need a snapshot of the composition to answer such queries. Local queries can be answered by directly querying the concerned provider as long as it provides a query interface like Web Services Distributed Management (WSDM) [WSDM].

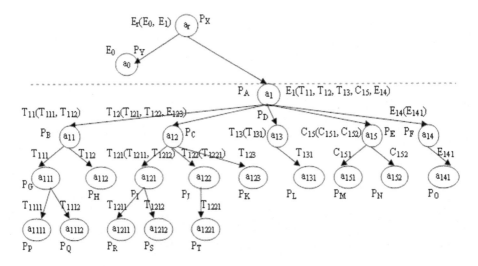

Fig. 10. Acquiring actual states of sub-trees

- Status queries: Queries expressed over the states of several providers. We assume that any query related to the status of a composition is expressed as a conjunction of the states of individual providers. Examples of status queries: "Have providers A, B and C reached states T, E and E respectively?", "Have providers A, B, C and D started executing?", etc. Status queries can be answered using snapshots acquired by any of the earlier given algorithms. Such queries have been referred to as stable predicates in literature. Stable predicates are defined as predicates which do not become false once they have become true. In our case, the stability of the query is reflected by the fact that we do not have to capture the state of a provider as E to conclude that it has started executing. We can infer the same even if the state of the provider is recorded as T/CI/ICI/CP/C/IS/S.

- History queries: Queries related to the execution history of the composition. For example, "How many times have providers A and B been suspended?". Both synchronized and actual state snapshots can be used to answer history related queries. A DSW snapshot cannot be used directly because the recorded states of the providers reflect their states at different times. If the query is answered using a snapshot acquired by the actual state algorithm then it needs to be mentioned that the statistics are with respect to a time t_p in the past.

– Relationship queries: Queries based on the relationship between states. For example, "What was the state of provider A when provider B was in E?", "Did provider A start executing before provider B?". Unfortunately, snapshot based mechanisms do not guarantee answers for such queries. For example, we would not be able to answer the first query unless we have a snapshot which captures the state of provider B when it was in state E. B could have been in state NE when a snapshot was taken and in state T when the next snapshot was taken. Such predicates have been referred to as unstable predicates in literature. Unstable predicates keep alternating their values between true and false. While unstable predicates are in general very difficult to detect, researchers have studied some special classes of unstable properties. (a) Strong unstable predicates [GW96] or predicates which will "definitely" hold [CM91]: A predicate is called a strong predicate if and only if the global state over which it holds is guaranteed to occur for any execution (irrespective of the execution speeds, communication delays and other variable parameters in a distributed setting). Intuitively, strong unstable predicates allow us to verify that a desirable state will always occur. (b) Strong unstable linked predicates [GW96], [MC88]: A linked predicate is expressed as a sequence of local predicates and is called a strong unstable linked predicate if the corresponding local states occur in the same sequence for every execution. Such predicates are useful in detecting the occurrence of a sequence of states in a distributed setting. We refer the reader to [SM92] for a survey of the unstable predicates studied in literature. In a hierarchical composition scenario, these special classes of unstable predicates help us in answering relationship queries as long as there exists a parent-child (ancestor-descendent) relationship between the concerned providers. For example, a global state where parent and child providers are executing simultaneously will definitely occur (strong) or an ancestor will always starting executing before any of its descendents (strong linked).

4   Conclusion and Future Work

Our objective in this paper is capturing the state of a hierarchical composition at a given point of time. Towards that end, we provided algorithms: (1) based on the assumption of synchronized clocks and (2) extension of the DSA (DSW). We outlined how the DSW can be customized to record the state of a part of the composition and optimized for taking successive snapshots. Then, we showed how we can acquire an actual state of the hierarchical composition given a DSW snapshot. Finally, we discussed using the captured state information to answer execution status related queries.

In future, we would like to extend the monitoring algorithms to consider failure detection including deadlocks, livelocks, etc. As discussed earlier, the DSW snapshot represents a consistent (rather than actual) state of the hierarchical composition. We are working towards a measure which would allow us to precisely quantify the difference between a DSW snapshot and an actual state, i.e., a measure of the accuracy of a DSW snapshot. The aspects discussed in this paper assume a static composition and dynamic binding environment. It would be interesting to try and apply the same to fully dynamic compositions.

Acknowledgements

We would like to thank the anonymous referees for their valuable comments which helped to improve the work in this paper considerably.

References

[B04]   Janusz Borkowski. Hierarchical Detection of Strongly Consistent Global States. In Proceedings of the 3rd International Symposium on Parallel and Distributed Computing, 2004, pp: 256-261.

[CL85]   K. M. Chandy and L. Lamport. Distributed Snapshots: Determining Global States of Distributed Systems. ACM Transactions on Computer Systems, 3(1):63-75, February 1985.

[CM91]   R. Cooper and K. Marzullo. Consistent detection of global predicates. In Proceedings of the ACM/ONR Workshop on Parallel Distributed Debugging 1991, pp: 163-173.

[GW96]   V.K. Garg and B.Waldecker. Detection of Strong Unstable Predicates in Distributed Programs. IEEE Trans. Parallel and Distributed Systems, Dec. 1996, pp: 1323-1333.

[L78]   L. Lamport. Time, Clocks and Ordering of Events in Distributed Systems. Comm. ACM, vol. 21, no. 7, pp: 558-565, July 1978.

[LAP03]   A. Lazovik, M. Aiello and M. Papazoglou. Planning and Monitoring the Execution of Web Service Requests. In Proceedings of the 1st International Conference on Service-Oriented Computing (ICSOC'03), 2003, LNCS 2910, pp: 335-350.

[M89]   F. Mattern. Virtual time and global states of distributed systems. In Parallel and Distributed Algorithms, Elsevier Science Publishers B.V. (North-Holland), 1989, pp: 215-226.

[M91]   D. L. Mills. Internet time synchronization: the Network Time Protocol. IEEE Trans. Communications 39, 10 (October 1991), pp: 1482-1493.

[MC88]   B.P. Miller and J.D. Choi. Breakpoints and Halting in Distributed Programs. In Proceedings of the 8th International Conference on Distributed Computing Systems, 1988, CS Press, pp: 316-323.

[PBBST04]   M. Pistore, P. Bertoli, F. Barbon, D. Shaparau and P. Traverso. Planning and Monitoring Web Service Composition. In Proceedings of the Workshop on Planning and Scheduling for Web and Grid Services, 2004.

[SM92]   R. Schwartz and F. Mattem. Detecting causal relationships in distributed computations: In search of the holy grail. Tech. Rep. SFB124- 15/92, Univ. of Kaiserslautern, Germany, 1992.

[V89]   S. Venkatesan. Message-optimal incremental snapshots. In Proceedings of the 9th International Conference on Distributed Computing Systems, 1989, pp: 53-60.

[WSA]   WS Security Addendum. http://msdn.microsoft.com/library/en-us/dnglobspec/ html/ws-security-addendum.asp.

[WSDM]   Specification: Web Services Distributed Management (WSDM). http:// devresource.hp. com/drc/specifications/wsdm/index.jsp.

Efficient Scheduling Strategies for Web Services-Based E-Business Transactions

Erdogan Dogdu[1] and Venkata Mamidenna[2]

[1] TOBB Economics and Technology University,
Computer Engineering Department, Ankara, Turkey
edogdu@etu.edu.tr
http://www.etu.edu.tr/~edogdu
[2] Georgia State University, Computer Science Department,
Atlanta, Georgia, USA
maswaroop@yahoo.com

Abstract. Web services platform, strongly backed by the information technology industry, is destined to change the software application integration, application interoperability, and distributed computing in radical ways. Web services platform is based on open data communication and data formatting protocols; therefore it has a very promising future in terms of adoptability. Future distributed applications in general and e-business applications in particular will be built rapidly by reusing web services components that are made available on Internet. These applications will talk to each other and utilize each other's functionality. This is in general called Service-Oriented Computing. For the service-oriented applications Quality of Service (QoS) will be a major concern considering the dependency over remote applications and Internet communication. In this paper we consider a service-oriented computing (e.g., e-business) environment where "similar" services are provided by many providers. Therefore, service clients can choose any of these service providers during run-time. Transactions (client programs that request services from multiple providers) are processed via "web services monitors" that handle service composition execution. Transaction monitor in this case need to efficiently schedule service requests to the best service provider in order to optimize the system throughput. We present some basic strategies for efficient scheduling of web services transactions. We show through a simulation-based evaluation that even basic strategies improve the system throughput substantially.

1 Introduction

Future software applications will be more web-enabled utilizing ubiquitous Internet protocols. Applications will be developed by reusing web-based components where remote applications will provide functionality over Web Services-based messaging protocols. Web Services-based interoperability will be the key communication infrastructure for building open, component-based, integrated web applications. Web Services enable heterogeneous software applications to communicate via XML-based messages. Applications in this framework can find web services providers, can be

C. Bussler and M.-C. Shan (Eds.): TES 2005, LNCS 3811, pp. 113–125, 2006.

integrated with the web services automatically, and use their services at runtime instantly, therefore providing interoperability. E-business and e-commerce applications in particular will be the showcase areas benefiting from this infrastructure.

There is also a concern in the area of transmitting and processing XML messages. XML files are larger in size compared to binary-coded and untagged data. Therefore, the transmission of large XML-tagged data over the network is slower than transmitting data with other formats. For the service-oriented applications Quality of Service (QoS) will be a major concern considering the dependency over remote applications and Internet communication [15]. Disconnections or unpredictable remote service availability will result in fluctuating performance behavior for web services-based applications. In addition to these, remotely used web services will be overloaded with many requests in some cases; this is similar to the web sites were overloaded in the early days of Internet and more scalable solutions are developed later on [1]. This will cause delays in getting services and therefore will cost the web services-dependent applications to suffer from slow response times.

Above mentioned performance concerns will be especially important for e-business and e-commerce applications due to the business nature of the applications. Some of these services are expected to be pay-per-use services, thus having monetary and profit-oriented end results.

Therefore, remote web services should be scalable and robust, handling overload conditions and responding to failures efficiently (transactional). Performance is therefore a major issue for WS-based applications or compositions (transactions).

Current web services-based application composition techniques only concentrate on (1) languages to compose WS invocations, (2) tools to generate composition scripts, and (3) engines to interpret and execute WS transactions. Next issue in this area will be developing scalable, robust, reliable, and performance-oriented execution of web services compositions or transactions. In this paper, we address the issue of QoS for web services transactions. We propose a two-step scheduling technique for dynamic execution of web services transactions. Specifically, we propose a new model for the composition and execution of web services-based transactions. In this model, we envision that future web services will provide "similar" services; therefore the clients of these services will be able to pick and choose from a selection list of services at runtime. In our proposal, a Web Services Monitor (WSM) handles the execution of web services transactions. WSM automatically searches service directories, finds, and executes a web service upon a request during runtime. WSM employs some basic scheduling schemes for the selection of web service providers when executing web service requests of transactions. We experimentally evaluate our WSM proposal and the service scheduling schemes via simulation and present some preliminary results at the end.

2   Web Services Monitor

We propose a new framework for efficient execution of web services compositions. In this framework, Web Services Monitors play an important role. A Web Services Monitor (WSM) is an execution engine for web services compositions and transactions [2].

WS transactions are submitted to a WSM and the WSM executes the transaction by interpreting the script that defines the process, for example an e-commerce transaction.

Many web services composition schemes and languages have been developed in recent years. Among those Business Process Execution Language for Web Services (BPEL4WS) specification, proposed by IBM, BEA, Microsoft and other industry leaders, is likely to become an industry standard [3]. A future implementation of our WSM will employ BPEL as the scripting language for web services transactions.

WSM in our proposal is not only a simple execution engine as seen in other composition execution engines such as BPWS4J from IBM, BPEL Server from Collaxa, and BEA's WebLogic Workshop. WSM is an intelligent execution engine with Quality of Service (QoS) considerations. QoS features include service selection, scheduling, preemption, load balancing, timely execution of transactions, etc.

In the early days of the Web, web servers became overloaded as the web usage increased dramatically. This resulted in scalable, distributed web server architectures [1]. We will see a similar trend for web services in the near future, as web services becoming the common integration solution for distributed, component- and service-oriented application development on the web. Future web services need to be more scalable, intelligently handling and rerouting web service requests during runtime. Our WSM is a step towards this direction.

WSM assumes that multiple service providers with the same or similar interfaces provide the same services of interest. For example, the following two web services provide stock quote service:

- http://www.xignite.com/xrealtime.asmx (GetRealQuote operation)
- http://66.28.98.121:9090/soap (getQuote operation)

First service has a method called "GetRealQuote" and the second service has a method called "getQuote". Both methods return the stock value for a given stock symbol. Therefore, a web service transaction that needs to find stock quote values can invoke any one of these two services.

Current web service composition languages incorporate "static" service selection features. This means services are selected during compile time and once services are determined, they cannot be changed until the transaction script is changed (another composition). For example in BPEL4WS, the BPEL script lists outside web services that will be used by the executable process (orchestration). Figure 1 shows an incomplete BPEL script depicting a travel reservation scenario [4].

In this example, the web service composition is utilizing two remote web services DeltaAirlines and MarriottHotels. It is a static composition of the specified two services. This travel reservation script makes reservations only from Delta Airlines and from Marriott Hotels but nowhere else.

In the future, a web services composition is supposed to specify the "type" of services needed in the composition, not some specific services. This way the composition will be more flexible and more robust, handling future changes in service providers (due to price, availability, service quality, etc.) much better than a static composition. Of course, this will not be the case for all service compositions; some compositions may still be needed to put together with static calls, for example due to contacts with certain service providers. But, a "dynamic" service selection and integration in runtime will be a needed feature for many service compositions.

```
<process name="TravelService"
    targetNamespace="http://tobb.com/bpel/travel/"
    xmlns="http://schemas.xmlsoap.org/ws/2003/03/
            business-process/"
    xmlns:bpws="http://schemas.xmlsoap.org/ws/2003/03/
                business-process/"
    xmlns:trv="http://tobb.com/bpel/travel/"
    xmlns:htl="http://tobb.com/service/hotel/"
    xmlns:aln="http://tobb.com/service/airline/" >

    <partnerLinks>
        ...
        <partnerLink name="DeltaAirlines"
                    partnerLinkType="aln:flightLT"
                    myRole="airlineCustomer"
                    partnerRole="airlineService"/>
        <partnerLink name="MarriottHotels"
                    partnerLinkType="htl:hotelLT"
                    myRole="hotelairlineCustomer"
                    partnerRole="hotelService"/>
        ...
    </partnerLinks>
    <variables>
        ...
        <variable name="FlightDetails"
            messageType="aln:FlightTicketRequestMessage"/>
        <variable name="HotelStayDetails"
            messageType="htl:HotelStayRequestMessage"/>
        ...
    </variables>
    <sequence>
        <flow>
            ...
            <sequence>
                <invoke partnerLink="DeltaAirlines"
                    portType="aln:FlightAvailabilityPT"
                    operation="FlightAvailability"
                    inputVariable="FlightDetails" />
                ...
            </sequence>
            <sequence>
                <invoke partnerLink="MarriottHotels"
                    portType="htl:HotelAvailabilityPT"
                    operation="HotelAvailability"
                    inputVariable="HotelStayDetails" />
                ...
            </sequence>
        </flow>
    </sequence>
</process>
```

Fig. 1. BPEL script of an executable process showing a travel web service

WSM we propose incorporates such a feature. While interpreting the transaction script, WSM also selects appropriate service providers among a number of
similar service providers for execution. Figure 2 depicts such a scenario for a web service

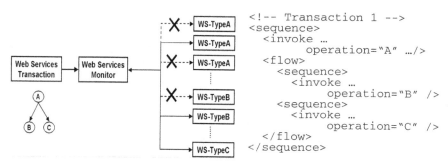

```
<!-- Transaction 1 -->
<sequence>
    <invoke …
        operation="A" …/>
    <flow>
        <sequence>
            <invoke …
                operation="B" />
        <sequence>
            <invoke …
                operation="C" />
    </flow>
</sequence>
```

Fig. 2. A web services transaction and the invocation of web services requests by WSM

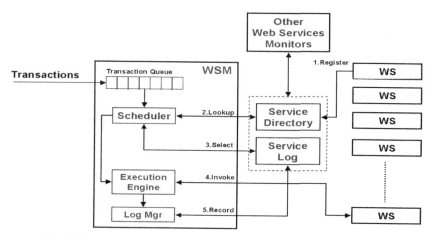

Fig. 3. Scheduling web services transactions via web services monitors

transaction consisting of 3 web service method invocations (A, B, and C). A number of web services are assumed to provide similar methods for each method type (A, B, C). During execution, WSM selects one of the available services for executing method A, then for method B and method C.

Figure 3 illustrates how a WSM works. WSM includes the following modules:

Service Directory: Service Directory is a central registry of service providers. Services are listed in this registry by their methods and their interfaces. Services are registered in the Service Directory as they become available. This can be done by an expert user or by the service developers who have appropriate privileges for registering services. Methods in each service are picked and grouped by their similarity and a search function is provided for clients. For example, the stock quote methods listed in the previous section are listed as two entries, one service point for each. A transaction (or client) interested in running one of the two methods can find the other using the service directory search function.

Transaction Queue: Many clients can send transactions concurrently to a WSM for execution. Therefore, transactions that are submitted to a WSM are first entered into the transaction queue for better scheduling, resource management and utilization reasons. Different WSMs can use different queuing mechanisms such as first-in-first-out, or priority queues such as real-time deadline or slack time-based queues. Scheduler in the WSM picks transactions from the queue for execution in the order they are supposed to be executed as resources (e.g., CPU, disk, etc.) become available.

Scheduler: Scheduler is an important module in WSM. It retrieves transactions from the transaction queue and executes them. During execution, as service method invocations are requested, scheduler looks up in the service directory for similar services providing similar methods. Then, the scheduler picks an appropriate service provider for the requested method invocation based on a number of criteria (see following sections). Scheduler uses "service log" for service selection using previous executions outcomes such as response times, etc. Upon selection of the service provider, method invocation is submitted in the form of a SOAP message by the execution engine in cooperation with the scheduler. While doing this, scheduler does not pick a different service provider in each new invocation within the same process. Once a service provider is selected, subsequent service invocations are directed to the same provider.

Execution Engine: This module is responsible for executing transactions and requesting method invocations from selected web services. It also talks to the log manager for recording appropriate outcomes that will be used by future web service transaction executions.

Log Manager: Log manager records the transaction outcomes in the central service log. These outcomes include the following and more: average response time and variation of response time for a specific method invocation (based on the number of previous executions of the same method).

In the framework we propose web services transactions are executed as follows:

Step 1. Register services and their methods in the service directory as they become available.

Transactions are submitted to a WSM. Transaction is first queued in the transaction queue of the WSM. Later scheduler picks transactions from queue based on transaction order and resource availability.

Step 2. Scheduler executes the transaction in cooperation with the execution engine. Scheduler "searches" the service directory and finds service providers that provide similar services that are requested by the transaction.

Step 3. Before invocation of a web service method, scheduler "selects" a service among a number of available ones that are found in step 2. For this, scheduler consults with "service log", and using a number of criteria implemented in the scheduler, selects an appropriate service provider.

Step 4. Execution engine, upon a request from scheduler, invokes the remote method in the selected service provider.

Step 5. The log manager upon a request from execution engine records service invocation outcomes, such as response time, in the service log. This happens after the response is taken from service provider.

3 Scheduling of Web Services Requests

Scheduling jobs among a number of parallel machines is a well-known problem. Most scheduling problems consider offline scheduling of a number of submitted jobs. Most of the scheduling problems are NP-Hard [5].

Web services are independently developed and managed entities. Therefore, they cannot be strictly controlled and services cannot be utilized in a controlled manner. Web service invocations will happen randomly at will whenever transactions are submitted to WSM and executed concurrently. Thus, scheduling web service transactions cannot be done offline. Web service transaction execution is an online scheduling problem.

Graham studied the online job-scheduling problem. He developed a simple and elegant solution for near-optimal scheduling of online jobs [6]. In Graham's online scheduling problem a number of jobs are to be scheduled on m identical parallel machines. The goal is to minimize the makespan of these jobs (completion time of the last job). The processing time of each job is known in advance. Graham's algorithm simply schedules the next job in line on the machine with the smallest load. There are variations of this algorithm adapted for different load characteristics [18].

We adapt a similar solution for our web services monitor. We propose some basic schemes for service provider selection and these are presented in the following section. A more comprehensive discussion of scheduling problems in our proposal is presented in [13]. There we discussed a very general framework where service executions are handled by many monitors (service composition execution engines) and compositions are first scheduled to an appropriate engine, and the engine dynamically schedules service request consequently (therefore called, two-step scheduling mechanism).

4 WSM Simulation

Since we are interested in the performance of scheduling strategies of WSM, we implemented a simulator to observe the performance of scheduling algorithms we propose. Our simulator is implemented using SimJava, which is a popular open-source discrete-event simulation development kit [12]. SimJava consists of a collection of Java libraries for building customized discrete-event simulators.

Our WSM simulator simulates the behavior of a single WSM. Therefore, only the second step of the two-step scheduling scheme we presented in the previous section is implemented. But, considering that both steps are dealing with the "load balancing" issue, similar techniques will apply to solve the optimization problem in each step. Anyhow, we will later include the first step scheduling in our solution, first in the simulator and then in a prototype implementation in future. Here, load balancing refers to the issue from a client's point of view. By distributing the web service calls among a number of servers evenly (by considering the server loads) will shorten the response times for clients' processes (compositions). On the other hand, servers will also benefit from this by getting a balanced load (server side improvement on processing times).

4.1 Scheduling Techniques Implemented

Our WSM simulator implements the following basic scheduling schemes, some of which we briefly discussed in previous sections:

a) **No Directory:** This is the base scheme that has no specific scheduling strategy. It will be used to compare against the other scheduling strategies. In this "No Dictionary" technique, we do not utilize web service provider similarities. Therefore, the web service directory in our system is not used at all. Each web service is considered as a unique service and therefore service requests in a transaction are directed to the specified web service provider.

b) **Round-Robin Scheduling:** In this scheme, similar web services are grouped and ordered in a list. Web service directory in figure 3 helps in this algorithm. Each entry in the directory consists of a number of similar services and their providers. These services are then ordered. During run-time, when there is a request for a web service, algorithm checks the entry in the directory for the requested service. Directory keeps a sliding pointer on each list of similar services (directory entries) and gives out the next service in line when requested and the slides the pointer to the next service in the list. This is basically the well-known "round-robin" scheduling technique from operating systems.

c) **Load Balancing:** We refine the previous round-robin scheduling technique with a load-balancing technique. We assume that in future web services will be very common and overload conditions on service providers will be likely (like it is the case with web servers time to time). Therefore, a load balancing technique will help to improve the overall server utilization and system throughput in cases where the system overload is very high (many transactions flooding service providers). We choose a simple method here. We use the same data structures as in the round-robin scheduling technique above. We add one more data: for each web services provider in a list, we also save the number of transactions being served by that provider. When the next service request comes, the service directory provides the server that is currently serving the least number of transactions among similar providers. This will basically distribute the hits among similar service providers, therefore improving the response times and therefore the transaction completion times.

4.2 Simulator Design

Figure 4 depicts the modular design of our system. System consists of the following modules:

Transaction Generator: This module generates a new transaction at certain intervals. The delay between contiguous transaction arrivals (generations) is exponentially distributed to model a near real environment.

Engine: Engine executes a transaction. A transaction consists of local processing operations and web services calls (mixed and sequential). Local processing involves CPU processing for computation and Disk access for read/write operations. Web service calls in the transaction are requests from web service providers. These calls

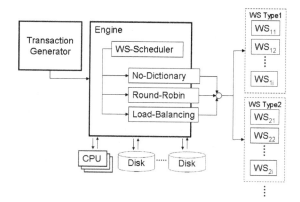

Fig. 4. Simulation system modules

Table 1. Simulation System Parameters

Parameter	Explanation	Test Run Values
NumberOfTx	Number of Transactions	200
MaxOpsTx	Maximum number of operations per tx	20
MinOpsTx	Minimum number of operations per tx	10
RateWSPerTx	Percentage of WS calls per tx	50%
RateCPUPerTx	Percentage of CPU operations per tx	20%
RateDiskPerTx	Percentage of Disk operations per tx	30%
ExecTimeWS	Average WS call execution time (ms)	30 ms (mean) 5 ms (variance)
ExecTimeCPU	Average CPU op. execution time (ms)	10 ms (mean) 2 ms (variance)
ExecTimeDisk	Average Disk op. execution time (ms)	15 ms (mean) 3 ms (variance)
TxArrivalRate	Intertransaction arrival rate (ms)	10-300ms
NumberOfWS	Number of Web Service Providers	50
NumberOfWSTypes	Number of Web Service Provider Types	15

require the transaction to wait for the web service response to come back before continuing. When a web service call is met Engine sends the request to one of the service providers according to one of the scheduling schemes. Engine implements the three basic scheduling schemes explained above, namely No-Dictionary, Round-Robin, and Load-Balancing. During experimental runs, a specific experiment can set the scheduling scheme to one of these.

Web Service Providers: These are the service providers independent of WSM. WSM Engine can use these when transactions request a service. They are grouped into similar service providers (service type). They imitate the behavior of executing a web service call by delaying for a specified number of milliseconds.

For the generation and execution of WS transactions, our simulator uses the parameters listed in Table 1. Parameters in the table are listed in a configuration table and the simulation system read those parameters to perform a test. System generates *NumberOfTx* transactions per experimental run. For each transaction, system generates between *MinOpsTx* and *MaxOpsTx* operations which is a uniformly distributed random number. *RateWSPerTx* percentage of operations are WS calls, the rest of the operations are CPU (*RateCPUPerTx*) and Disk (*RateDiskPerTx*) operations (local processing operations). WS calls take in average *ExecTimeWS* ms to execute, CPU operations take in average *ExecTimeCPU* ms, and Disk operations take in average *ExecTimeDisk* ms. These are normally distributed random variables. The delay between two consecutive transaction generations is exponentially distributed with the mean *TxArrivalRate*. There are a fixed number of WS providers (*NumberOfWS*) and a fixed number of WS types (*NumberOfWSTypes*) these WS providers belong to.

5 Experimental Results

Third column in Table 1 lists the values we used in the experiments for the configuration parameters. Figure 5 lists some early results. According to the results presented in Figure 5, both RR and LB perform much better than ND scheme. That is, both schemes lower the average execution time of transactions in the system. Simply, higher throughput is obtained in the system. Therefore, we conclude that even basic service selection algorithms will result in better system throughput, i.e. higher number of transaction executions and completions, better utilization of system resources and service providers.

In between the two basic schemes, RR and LB, we obtained that LB performs slightly better than RR. This is expected, but the difference is not too much as one might expect. This is due to the selection of system parameter values. In a system overload condition, this difference is expected to be larger since load balancing handles overload conditions better by distributing the load between servers.

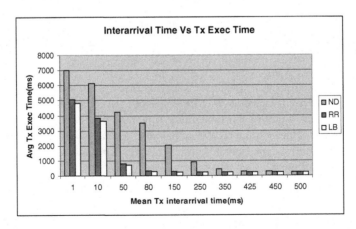

Fig. 5. Experimental results, comparing the average transaction (tx) execution time for 3 different scheduling schemes (ND: no-dictionary, RR: round-robin, LB: load-balancing)

6   Related Works

"Web services" is a new technology that is offering a new XML-based middleware for Internet-oriented application integration and distributed application development over heterogeneous devices and platforms [8][10]. Future use of web services in real e-business world requires transactional specification and execution mechanisms. Many works in this area are reported. Developing standards for web services composition and transactional execution is one of the interesting topics getting a lot of attention from both academia and industry [3][8][9].

Scheduling web services transactions is a new research area. There are not many work reported in the literature. SELF-SERVE is a related work in this area [7]. SELF-SERVE is a web services composition and scheduling tool. Its scheduling component mainly concentrates on optimal service selection for individual and isolated compositions. It also assumes that a-priori execution time of web service invocations is known in advance along with the cost of web service invocations [7]. In our work, we consider multiple compositions and their assignment to web services monitors and then assignment of individual web service invocations to web services providers (among a number of providers of similar services).

METEOR-S is another system developed at University of Georgia with a similar dynamic service binding concept [14]. METEOR-S provides static, deployment-time, and run-time service binding based on constraints associated with web processes. Their experiments show that run-time binding is very costly; response times are 7 times more than deployment-time binding, and almost 20 times more than static binding. This is' mainly due to the service discovery process. Our system differs from METEOR-S; our discovery process is much more robust than METEOR-S because we do offline evaluation of service providers and similar services are listed in a directory for run-time evaluation prior to execution. Therefore, there is no cost associated with the service discovery in our framework during runtime execution. We do not exercise a general purpose service discovery scheme, like the one used in METEOR-S or as it is envisioned in "semantic web services" research [16][17]. Instead, services are presorted and listed service directories with "type" information, and therefore the scheduler is bound to choose from a given list in our framework. We believe there will be place for both cases in a future e-business world: in some scenarios, contracts will be sought, and therefore similar services will be picked and listed in service directories (as in our case) and in some other scenarios, service composition will be free to pick and choose from anywhere within specified constraints (there might even be automatic negotiations).

7   Conclusions

In this paper we presented a new web services composition model where web services compositions utilize similar web services offerings during runtime via an execution engine. In this model, web services compositions are not strictly put together out of fixed web services (static model) but the composition specifies a flexible execution model (dynamic model). When submitted to a web service transaction execution engine (WSM), the engine chooses which web service to use during runtime. Therefore our model presents a better solution for performance-oriented use of web services.

Here, we are faced with a scheduling challenge in this model: WSM should make an intelligent choice among a number of similar web services to increase the system throughput. A simulation system developed and some of the basic scheduling schemes we developed for service selection are tested. Results show better system throughput even with these basic algorithms.

As a continuation of this work we will build a real Web Services Monitor that can be used to schedule web services transactions. This engine will be based on BPEL4WS specification, the latest language proposal for web services composition.

One more problem we did not address in this paper is how the service similarities will be determined. Even if two service providers provide similar services, there could be differences in service "signatures", such as service method names, input/output parameter types, counts, and ordering, etc. This is a "service matching" problem. "Semantic web services" research area tries to address this issue by attaching meaning to services using ontologies and how services could be picked, matched, and used dynamically [16][17]. This problem certainly needs to be addressed in a meaningful "automatic service selection and execution" framework. Our future work will also investigate this issue.

References

1. Aversa, L., Bestavros, A., "Load Balancing a Cluster of Web Servers Using Distributed Packet Rewriting", Proc. of IEEE Int. Performance, Computing, and Comm. Conf., 2000.
2. Dogdu, E., "An Extended Web Services Framework", Proc. of the IASTED Int. Conf. on Communications, Internet and Information Technology, 2002.
3. BPEL4WS - Specification: Business Process Execution Language for Web Services Version 1.1. See: http://www-106.ibm.com/developerworks/webservices/library/ws-bpel/.
4. Sample BPEL scripts, see: http://www.sys-con.com/webservices/sourcec.cfm.
5. Carrey, M.R., Johnson D.S., Computers and Intractability: A Guide to the Theory of NP-Completeness. W.H. Freeman, 1979.
6. Graham, R.L., "Bounds for certain multi-processing anomalies". Bell System Tech. Journal, 45:1563-1581, 1966.
7. Zeng, L., Benatallah, B., Dumas, M., Kalagnanam, J., Sheng, Q. Z., "Quality Driven WS Composition", Proc. Of the World Wide Web Conference, 2003.
8. Peltz, C., "Web Services Orchestration and Choreography", IEEE Computer, Oct 2003.
9. Little, M., "Transactions and Web Services", Communication of the ACM, Oct 2003.
10. Dogdu, E., Sunderraman, R., "A Web Services Testing Tool", Proc. of the 7th IASTED Int. Conf. on Internet and Multimedia Systems and Applications, Aug 13-15, 2003.
11. Mamidenna, V., "Efficient Scheduling Strategies for Web Service Transactions", M.S. Thesis, Georgia State University, 2004.
12. SimJava, see: http://www.dcs.ed.ac.uk/home/hase/simjava/
13. Dogdu, E., "Scheduling Web Services Transactions", Proc. of the 2004 International Symposium on Web Services and Applications (ISWS'04), 2004, Las Vegas, Nevada, USA.
14. Verma, K., Gomadam, K., Sheth, A. P., Miller, J. A., Wu, Z., "The METEOR-S Approach for Configuring and Executing Dynamic Web Processes", Large Scale Distributed Information Systems Lab. University of Georgia. Technical Report 05-001, 2005.

15. Menasce, D.A., "Quality of Service Issues in Web Services", IEEE Internet Computing, 6(6), 72-75, 2002.
16. Semantic web-enabled web services. http://swws.semanticweb.org
17. Semantic web services. http://www.daml.org/services
18. Susanne Albers, Bianca Schröder, "An Experimental Study of Online Scheduling Algorithms", Journal of Experimental Algorithms, 7(3), 1-14, 2002.

Author Index

Lecture Notes in Computer Science

For information about Vols. 1–3773

please contact your bookseller or Springer

Vol. 3819: P. Van Hentenryck (Ed.), Practical Aspects of Declarative Languages. X, 231 pages. 2005.

Vol. 3818: S. Grumbach, L. Sui, V. Vianu (Eds.), Advances in Computer Science – ASIAN 2005. XIII, 294 pages. 2005.

Vol. 3817: M. Faundez-Zanuy, L. Janer, A. Esposito, A. Satue-Villar, J. Roure, V. Espinosa-Duro (Eds.), Nonlinear Analyses and Algorithms for Speech Processing. XII, 380 pages. 2006. (Sublibrary LNAI).

Vol. 3816: G. Chakraborty (Ed.), Distributed Computing and Internet Technology. XXI, 606 pages. 2005.

Vol. 3815: E.A. Fox, E.J. Neuhold, P. Premsmit, V. Wuwongse (Eds.), Digital Libraries: Implementing Strategies and Sharing Experiences. XVII, 529 pages. 2005.

Vol. 3814: M. Maybury, O. Stock, W. Wahlster (Eds.), Intelligent Technologies for Interactive Entertainment. XV, 342 pages. 2005. (Sublibrary LNAI).

Vol. 3813: R. Molva, G. Tsudik, D. Westhoff (Eds.), Security and Privacy in Ad-hoc and Sensor Networks. VIII, 219 pages. 2005.

Vol. 3811: C. Bussler, M.-C. Shan (Eds.), Technologies for E-Services. VIII, 127 pages. 2006.

Vol. 3810: Y.G. Desmedt, H. Wang, Y. Mu, Y. Li (Eds.), Cryptology and Network Security. XI, 349 pages. 2005.

Vol. 3809: S. Zhang, R. Jarvis (Eds.), AI 2005: Advances in Artificial Intelligence. XXVII, 1344 pages. 2005. (Sublibrary LNAI).

Vol. 3808: C. Bento, A. Cardoso, G. Dias (Eds.), Progress in Artificial Intelligence. XVIII, 704 pages. 2005. (Sublibrary LNAI).

Vol. 3807: M. Dean, Y. Guo, W. Jun, R. Kaschek, S. Krishnaswamy, Z. Pan, Q.Z. Sheng (Eds.), Web Information Systems Engineering – WISE 2005 Workshops. XV, 275 pages. 2005.

Vol. 3806: A.H. H. Ngu, M. Kitsuregawa, E.J. Neuhold, J.-Y. Chung, Q.Z. Sheng (Eds.), Web Information Systems Engineering – WISE 2005. XXI, 771 pages. 2005.

Vol. 3805: G. Subsol (Ed.), Virtual Storytelling. XII, 289 pages. 2005.

Vol. 3804: G. Bebis, R. Boyle, D. Koracin, B. Parvin (Eds.), Advances in Visual Computing. XX, 755 pages. 2005.

Vol. 3803: S. Jajodia, C. Mazumdar (Eds.), Information Systems Security. XI, 342 pages. 2005.

Vol. 3802: Y. Hao, J. Liu, Y.-P. Wang, Y.-m. Cheung, H. Yin, L. Jiao, J. Ma, Y.-C. Jiao (Eds.), Computational Intelligence and Security, Part II. XLII, 1166 pages. 2005. (Sublibrary LNAI).

Vol. 3801: Y. Hao, J. Liu, Y.-P. Wang, Y.-m. Cheung, H. Yin, L. Jiao, J. Ma, Y.-C. Jiao (Eds.), Computational Intelligence and Security, Part I. XLI, 1122 pages. 2005. (Sublibrary LNAI).

Vol. 3799: M. A. Rodríguez, I.F. Cruz, S. Levashkin, M.J. Egenhofer (Eds.), GeoSpatial Semantics. X, 259 pages. 2005.

Vol. 3798: A. Dearle, S. Eisenbach (Eds.), Component Deployment. X, 197 pages. 2005.

Vol. 3797: S. Maitra, C. E. V. Madhavan, R. Venkatesan (Eds.), Progress in Cryptology - INDOCRYPT 2005. XIV, 417 pages. 2005.

Vol. 3796: N.P. Smart (Ed.), Cryptography and Coding. XI, 461 pages. 2005.

Vol. 3795: H. Zhuge, G.C. Fox (Eds.), Grid and Cooperative Computing - GCC 2005. XXI, 1203 pages. 2005.

Vol. 3794: X. Jia, J. Wu, Y. He (Eds.), Mobile Ad-hoc and Sensor Networks. XX, 1136 pages. 2005.

Vol. 3793: T. Conte, N. Navarro, W.-m.W. Hwu, M. Valero, T. Ungerer (Eds.), High Performance Embedded Architectures and Compilers. XIII, 317 pages. 2005.

Vol. 3792: I. Richardson, P. Abrahamsson, R. Messnarz (Eds.), Software Process Improvement. VIII, 215 pages. 2005.

Vol. 3791: A. Adi, S. Stoutenburg, S. Tabet (Eds.), Rules and Rule Markup Languages for the Semantic Web. X, 225 pages. 2005.

Vol. 3790: G. Alonso (Ed.), Middleware 2005. XIII, 443 pages. 2005.

Vol. 3789: A. Gelbukh, Á. de Albornoz, H. Terashima-Marín (Eds.), MICAI 2005: Advances in Artificial Intelligence. XXVI, 1198 pages. 2005. (Sublibrary LNAI).

Vol. 3788: B. Roy (Ed.), Advances in Cryptology - ASIACRYPT 2005. XIV, 703 pages. 2005.

Vol. 3787: D. Kratsch (Ed.), Graph-Theoretic Concepts in Computer Science. XIV, 470 pages. 2005.

Vol. 3785: K.-K. Lau, R. Banach (Eds.), Formal Methods and Software Engineering. XIV, 496 pages. 2005.

Vol. 3784: J. Tao, T. Tan, R.W. Picard (Eds.), Affective Computing and Intelligent Interaction. XIX, 1008 pages. 2005.

Vol. 3783: S. Qing, W. Mao, J. Lopez, G. Wang (Eds.), Information and Communications Security. XIV, 492 pages. 2005.

Vol. 3782: K.-D. Althoff, A. Dengel, R. Bergmann, M. Nick, T.R. Roth-Berghofer (Eds.), Professional Knowledge Management. XXIII, 739 pages. 2005. (Sublibrary LNAI).

Vol. 3781: S.Z. Li, Z. Sun, T. Tan, S. Pankanti, G. Chollet, D. Zhang (Eds.), Advances in Biometric Person Authentication. XI, 250 pages. 2005.

Vol. 3780: K. Yi (Ed.), Programming Languages and Systems. XI, 435 pages. 2005.

Vol. 3779: H. Jin, D. Reed, W. Jiang (Eds.), Network and Parallel Computing. XV, 513 pages. 2005.

Vol. 3778: C. Atkinson, C. Bunse, H.-G. Gross, C. Peper (Eds.), Component-Based Software Development for Embedded Systems. VIII, 345 pages. 2005.

Vol. 3777: O.B. Lupanov, O.M. Kasim-Zade, A.V. Chaskin, K. Steinhöfel (Eds.), Stochastic Algorithms: Foundations and Applications. VIII, 239 pages. 2005.

Vol. 3776: S.K. Pal, S. Bandyopadhyay, S. Biswas (Eds.), Pattern Recognition and Machine Intelligence. XXIV, 808 pages. 2005.

Vol. 3775: J. Schönwälder, J. Serrat (Eds.), Ambient Networks. XIII, 281 pages. 2005.

Vol. 3774: G. Bierman, C. Koch (Eds.), Database Programming Languages. X, 295 pages. 2005.